ALSO BY SHANNON DENISE EVANS
Velvet Moon Chronicles: The Leveling

What the Mountains Know

LIFE, UNSTUCK

by Shannon Denise Evans

LAMPLIGHTER PUBLISHING HOUSE, LLC

NEW YORK

Lamplighter Publishing House
Lamplighter Publishing House, LLC
New York, New York

Content Editing: Michael Mendiola
Copyediting: Shayla Raquel
Cover Design: Christina Cucco, and Dragon House Creative, LTD.
Interior Formatting: The Frontispiece, *thefrontispiece.com*

This book is not intended as a substitute for the medical advice
of physicians. The reader should regularly consult a physician in
matters relating to his or her health and particularly with respect
to any symptoms that may require diagnosis or medical attention.

Graphics conceived by Shannon Denise Evans
Graphics designed by Shannon Denise Evans, Christina Cucco,
and Dragon House Creative, LTD.

Paperback: 978-0-9995351-0-3
Ebook: 978-0-9995351-1-0
Audio: 978-0-9995351-2-7

*This book is dedicated to my dear friend,
editor, and creative partner in crime,
Michael Mendiola.
Words cannot express my gratitude
for his talent, patience, and kindness.*

Contents

Preface

I AM A PERSON WHO SLOWLY AWOKE and found myself restless, yearning, and hungry. Although I am not a scientist, psychologist, or spiritualist, what I learned on my journey toward meeting myself and embodying my true expression is the impetus for creating this work and writing this book.

For the last ten years, I've been on a deeply personal path toward actualization—a journey rewarding in its ability to foster clarity and conscious living. If I'm honest, I didn't choose to step onto the path.

I was pushed.

I was thrust out of my comfort zone onto a path that has led me back to myself, and I wouldn't change or reverse the walk I've taken—and am continuing to take—for anything in the world.

Organically, I began noticing that people around me were gravitating toward their own respective paths and, in so doing, were longing for like-minded fellowship; comrades to walk with and among when they needed support. In seeing this trend increase exponentially,

3

specifically over the past few years, I began writing, coaching, and opening up my own experience as a way of bringing a sense of unity to those on this journey.

Between coaching others and my own personal experience, I've uncovered an absolute Universal truth: you are what resonates from deep within your being, the unique expression only you were given—one that rises up through the floor of your soul and sends shockwaves through your heart. You are gloriously and wonderfully made, and until you let in your resolute greatness, you will feel the constant pang of its absence. You are not other people's expectations. You are not the sum of all the parts thrust upon you, whether societal or familial. You are not a product of your environment. The only thing you are, is yours: you own you.

Within the pages of this book, you will find that through the world's deafening noise, there is a quiet space—a path that will lead you back to your soul. It is here that you can unify the fragmented particles of the stardust from which you are made, from which we are all made. You were created to make waves. You were created to whip up the wind. You were created to move mountains.

Introduction

THE PING

If you feel something's missing, it probably is. It starts as a quiet ping, then becomes deafening. Restlessness sets in, then listlessness. Things once fulfilling become mundane. But you can break free. You can learn to move mountains. And it's far simpler than you think.

HOME ALONE

First, understand that you are not alone. You are in a co-creative relationship with the most powerful Force in existence. And I truly mean a *Force*. It lives, breathes, and moves within you, outside you, and *for* you. It's a light in the darkness, a voice in the storm, and the echo of your soul: the seed of creation. It is, and functions as, a (and your) *You-niverse*.

Universe is a relative term that changes meaning based upon who's engaged in the conversation. Some feel it's God and God's respective playground; others may say it's simply empty space; many believe it's the echo and responsive liquidity of the Collective, our spirits all combining to form a super-conscious higher mind.

Regardless of how you define the immensity of the concept of time and space (or the Universe) is immaterial, seeing as it's seeded within you independent from the mental construct informing your view of the world around you. In learning more about the Grid Work (to be covered in a later chapter), we'll focus on the star-dusted Universal seed inside you and how it cultivates your relationship between you and your higher intellect.

Your *You-niverse* is the fundamental unified structure within which you incubate your truest expression. And it cannot, in any way, be divided. You and the Universal co-creative Force are bound in spirit, sinew, blood, and bone, all forged together by the Universe's ultimate expression of *Love*, or Light Originated Variant Energy—which is the fuel of creation.

This is not referencing a romanticized or commercial version of love; it's exploring the basis of all that we are: *Love* propels an initial electric pulse. That pulse seeks ionic density. Those ions attract creation energy. That energy becomes matter. And that matter becomes you. The nucleus of the message here is that you are part of a vast family of living things wrapped into the fabric of spatial formation, all of which desire to play with you, to create with you . . . and to *support* you.

The illusion of separation—or believing you are alone and / or not part of the larger structure—is one of

UNIVERSE
(liquidity of creation)

SOURCE

GRID
(energetic current of all that is)

COLLECTIVE
(consciousness of all that is)

UNIVERSAL FLOW
(energy in resonance)

the most dangerous myths you can adopt as your truth. It breeds *dis*-ease, which is a byproduct of repressed expression—*Love* without motion—and suffering, which is a byproduct of active resistance to the truth of who you are. How then does this play out in practical terms? By eventually, if left unaddressed, bringing you to your knees.

When you're locked inside the confines of your humanness (the mental/physical plane) and have neglected to include and/or call upon your limitlessness (the Universal plane), you will be in a constant state of lack—not because you don't deserve more, but because you don't *believe* you deserve more. When you are in union with primary Force and Universal truth, all that is will consistently conspire to manifest your highest good. In essence, believing *is* seeing.

HARNESSING THE ELEMENTS

Our bodies are oceanic in their makeup. Water is our lifeline and a primary conductor of electrical current. That current, when unable to flow, results in a state of inaction, or *that which must move* (energy/spirit) blocked by *that which is unmovable* (mind/will). This lack of flow translates to: the opposite of love is not hate, but rather, inaction.

The mind, with a healthy dose of urging from the ego, wants to keep us bound by the illusion of separation because it perceives unification with the Universe's Source as a loss of control.

The Essential Elements:
The Cardinal Points of Life

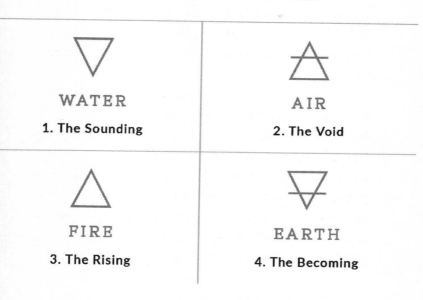

WATER

1. The Sounding

AIR

2. The Void

FIRE

3. The Rising

EARTH

4. The Becoming

Mostly, this is a leftover function of a primitive mind-set: "Total control over my environment means I won't die," or "Total control over my territory means my family won't die," or "If everyone stays inside my territory, we won't die." In modern terms, "inside the territory" can be replaced with "inside the mind." Fundamentally, the primitive mind does not seek exploration or new territory. Instead, the primitive mind believes small equals safe and that known trumps unknown.

SOURCE

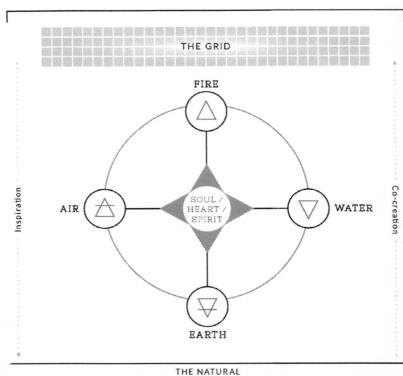

THE GRID

FIRE

AIR

SOUL /
HEART /
SPIRIT

WATER

EARTH

Inspiration

Co-creation

THE NATURAL

The primitive mindset demands that all elements be under its control. But the state of our being is to call forth the elements in co-creation. Control negates the sense of wonder and play necessary to manifest, which is where the distinction of love versus inaction becomes vital: manifestation of the mind is small and temporary; manifestation of the spirit is expansive and lasting.

Calling forth the elements and learning to balance them within you is your greatest asset—and challenge— as a human being. Unification and relationship with Source states: "As above, so below." Or more clearly, "The elements of the Universe reside within me, and I reside within the elements of the Universe."

It's important to understand that everyone has a driving element, one that is both vice and virtue depending on its state of balance. As an example, take an individual whose driving element is fire: they get things done, they fuel progress, and they light up the night. But if unbalanced, they can also burn themselves and others out, in turn creating drama or setting their lives ablaze.

Every minute of every day, we are managing a volatile ecosystem within and outside us: mind, ego, elements, Universal unity, spirit, will, heart, body— the list is endless. These items on their own can feel overwhelming, and we've yet to add the variables of *living* to the list. What happens when we add work, children, partners, and families? More often than not, the result is a lack of balance and in an environment without balance, our mind will go into lockdown. The primitive mindset takes control and our limitlessness is wrestled into the territory of *small equals safe*.

As a result, we end up stuck and paralyzed by inaction, where *that which must move* is blocked by *that which is unmovable*. Or that which was once open terrain is now a range of mountains. But what those mountains know and can teach us will unlock all that we are meant to be, if we only have the courage to listen and, more importantly, to seek their counsel.

The Sounding

ELEMENT: **WATER**

"The best thing one can do when
it's raining is to let it rain."
—Henry Wadsworth Longfellow

CHAPTER ONE

Learning to Carry Water

MANY YEARS AGO, my beloved mentor said, "Planning is priceless. Plans are useless." To me, this was an infuriating concept. If it hadn't been for the respect I had for her, I would have responded with: "What the actual &#%* does that *mean*, and how do I apply it in practical terms?"

Instead, I calmed the fire inside me and responded flatly, "I'm going to need more information."

With a jovial and infectious laugh, she replied, "It's better I don't explain. Your mind doesn't need to understand, because your soul does."

Continually, she would speak about the soul and its ever-present, solid, and unshakeable wisdom. What I soon came to learn was that the cord between conscious awareness and the soul is often crimped by the

15

madman dwelling in between our ears—in essence, the mind is not your friend. Does it have its place? Absolutely. Should it reign supreme in the hierarchy of *you*? Absolutely not.

PLANNING VS. PLANS

If we break down my mentor's words of wisdom, we have two components: planning and plans. *Planning* is a directive the mind can understand, as it identifies with a task: "I'm valuable because I'm planning." Giving the mind a job offers it a sense of purpose and keeps what would otherwise be a source of interference in check and focused. Most importantly, with the mind occupied, the heart (the soul's mouthpiece) has the opportunity to inform, inspire, and instill.

Plans is where things tend to veer off the rails, seeing as this involves the ego and its fervent, and sometimes brutal, quest for a permanent and defined identity. While the mind stays in an exploratory frame of planning—essentially, playing within the realm of what is possible—the ego—the maker of the plans—barges in and replaces exploration with a rigid, stone-constructed directive: *This* is the plan. *This* is what is going to happen. *This* is who you are.

With the soul's expansiveness of exploration now quashed and the ego's hardened regime in place, we can see how plans are counter-effective and, ultimately, useless. Why? Because there is no room for expression.

PLANS

Stagnancy & Calcification

BLOCK

NO OUTLET

States of Being:

"I Push." "I Hold." "I Must."

PLANNING

Flow of Co-Creation

States of Being:

"I Feel." "I Move." "I Wonder."

There is no path for curiosity's hungry feet. There is no space to live in wonderment.

Once bound by the confines of the plan your ego has forced upon you, you are—for all intents and purposes—unconscious. To be clear, I'm not using this term as it relates to the structure of traditional psychology. I'm using it as it relates to the principles of the Grid Work, which is the exploration of immersive self-awareness and activation of the Law of Amplitude.

Ego's plan has wrapped you in an identity whether you like it or not: "I'm the smart one"; "I'm the most talented"; "I'm the top of my class"; "I'm the hardest working"; "I'm the breadwinner"; "I'm the most sought after in my profession"; "I always win." The list goes on. When you're in an ego-wrangled unconscious state bent on making that identity true, you are constantly at the mercy of the biggest beast any of us will ever face: fear.

Fear will manifest consciously, or in the Natural (physical plane) in many forms, and in a range of varying intensities: a need to control, aversion to intimacy, anti/pro-risk behavior, over-functioning in perceived role(s), ruthless pursuit of assumed desires, addictive tendencies, lack of self-care, judgment of self/others, biting communication style, territorialism, shaming. Again, the list goes on.

Fear can also manifest in the Natural as a kind of paralysis or fog-like state: complacency, despondency, restlessness, purposelessness, longing, irritability, lack of inspiration, defensiveness, loneliness, joylessness, superiority, and so on.

Fear, at its base, has only one function: to keep you enslaved to the plan.

How does fear bind you? By perpetuating the illusion of separation. It's that little voice in your head ready to slap on labels or tell stories—often quite far from reality—about what's happening in any given situation: "He's/she's doing that on purpose"; "He's/she's trying to control me"; "He's/she's untrustworthy."

Now the ego has you right where it wants you: dependent upon it for your identity and supposed safety, which ultimately translates into a feeling of being trapped or stuck.

Yet you need not vilify the ego, seeing as within an equally weighted elemental structure, the ego has its place. The nucleus of the message is attaining balance: all the parts of you need a voice, most importantly, the soul. Listening to the soul takes courage and practice; it whispers, whereas the mind shouts and the ego screams. And the cacophony of sound—if left unchecked—eventually causes fatigue; and once you're exhausted, the ego and its plans easily take the reins.

Responsible plans are, of course, excluded from the framework of this topic, as it's advisable to plan your estate, retirement, living will, and other practical life matters. Specifically, the plans being referred to here are those containing absolutes, such as: "I must make partner / managing director / vice president by thirty-five"; "I have to buy a home by forty"; "I'll consider myself successful when _____"; "I'll be fulfilled if _____." It's these when/then and if/then plan drivers that block the current of our co-creative connection to not only the Universe, but also to our very selves.

What's crucial to remember is that you are not your ego's plans, and you are not separate: we are all in this together.

GO WHERE THE SUN DOESN'T SHINE

In truth, it's not about whether you're stuck, because most of us have either been stuck in the past or are currently stuck. It's whether you allow yourself to see it—to *feel* it. When you take time to analyze the plan that's been running your life, you may realize what your soul has been whispering to you all along: that it's out of step with, or counter to, who you actually are.

Most of us have pieces of our identities defined by goals, titles or achievements, but at what cost? For every false rose our plan identity has planted, there are three true roses just beneath it waiting to bloom in the forms of inspiration, imagination, and illumination. Who we are can only push up and through encrusted earth if we have the courage to first till the soil, and that may mean ripping up and mulching roses we've been tending to our entire lives.

Yet, know that those false roses have grown in an artificial environment—one heavily curated by what we want to see, what coincides with our plan, and what furthers our view of whom we *think* we are. This garden is tightly controlled, the sun always shining, the air overly perfumed; but if we get close enough, we'll most likely notice the petals look too perfect, like something manufactured willfully masquerading as real.

Breaking away from the plan requires first accepting that the plan is not who you are. Second, it's fundamental that you accept *what is*, which transforms into: "I am not my / my ego's plan(s)." This, in and of itself, is an irrefutable self-admission. You will feel a weight lifting up and away from you immediately, because you're surrendering to *what is* versus what *isn't*—that which is real versus that which is false.

With this step, you've started tilling soil, and more importantly, you've let in the rain. You've traded an artificial, ever-shining sun for the truth of a garden nourished by one of the most fundamental building blocks of life: water.

The power of giving yourself permission to awaken is profound and little by little, clarity will seep into your daily view. The Grid Work is subtle in that it *works* on you. The soil you've begun to mulch will slowly comingle with the elements and newfound nourishment being absorbed. In time, tiny seedlings will sprout—evidence that the soul again has a voice—and your mind can return to a state of play: planning to create, planning to align, planning to express.

Accepting *what is* doesn't mean waking up and finding yourself as a different person. It doesn't mean quitting a job, shirking responsibilities, or severing relationships; it's far subtler than that. What it allows for is letting go of that which no longer serves your higher purpose, your true expression, or your ability to summon and then carry your own water.

It is our given birthright to command the elements within us, each with its own fruit to bear. But those elements demand balance, and they deserve respect. To use them, you must understand them and to do that, you must first surrender to your true and natural state: honoring that which you are born to express.

Your soul knows who you are and in giving yourself the freedom to see *what is*, you begin tilling soil. You leave the falsity of what was and step into the grace of what can be. If you will stand in the fresh earth you've mustered the courage to mulch, even if only for a moment, you can open your heart, then let it rain.

HOW TO MOVE THE MOUNTAIN

Grid Focus: Self-assessment
Elemental Phase: I am but a drop of rain.

- Get still and breathe deeply until you can hear your own heartbeat clearly. You don't have to forcefully listen, as the sound will simply meet you where you are. Your heartbeat will slowly merge into your conscious awareness. Once you're still enough to hear it, move to the next step.

- Ask yourself: "Where am I in resistance?" Innately, you already know the answer to this, but the goal with this exercise is to bring the answer into your awareness without judgment or a need to *fix* or *act* upon anything you discover. Once you are aware of the area of resistance, move to the next step.

- Now, ask yourself to explore the *what is* that you are in resistance to. Move away from the urge to ask *why* you are in resistance, as it's not relevant. Instead, simply bring into your awareness *what is*. Once you feel this is clear, move to the next step.

- Gently tell yourself: "I'm willing and able to accept *what is*. It does not define me or control me." Repeat this silently to yourself until you feel the resistance leaving your awareness. Stick with the mantra and actively elect to let go of time while staying in harmony with the phrase until you're in an honest state of release.

CHAPTER TWO

The River Wild

OPENING YOUR AWARENESS to the *what is* that's causing resistance within you is a vital first step. But it's not
a magic pill. You may awaken enough to know you're
not living optimally or in alignment with that which you
wish to express. However, it takes far more excavation
to unearth the root cause of your willingness to allow a
state of resistance to have been—or to be—permeating
your life.

Slowly and thoroughly, we'll move toward unlocking
your unique expression, which will require *seeding*—the
careful introduction of specific concepts or ideas. Seeding
allows the concepts being highlighted to marinate under the radar (in the unconscious) away from the mind
and the ego's ever-ready surface-to-air missile defense

system. Once we're preparing to shift concept (idea) to creation (practice), we'll have a better chance of bypassing the mind's tendency to stagnate in resistance.

In that vein, there are two major themes to seed into your unconscious while in this period of dawning self-awareness: first, "Do I feel I deserve that which I'm driven to express?" and second, "Do I feel I can manifest that which I'm driven to express?" Breaking it down further, expression is what creates resonance, and resonance is what clears the way for expression and, ultimately, joy. As with all things in life, the map to expression flows circularly—it all starts and ends with you.

It's important to understand that in this context we are not, and should not be, confusing *deserve* with *entitlement*. In the Grid Work, to feel the current of *deserving* simply means you are accepting the goodness of that which the Universe, through Source connection, is holding in trust for you.

Expanding on this first theme: imagine you created a lightbulb of hand-blown glass with painstakingly spun golden filaments—a creation into which you've woven and molded the threads of your very soul. As the bulb's creator, would you then deny the bulb the right to an electric (Source) current, which would, in essence, allow it to shine, thereby fulfilling its purpose for having been created?

No, you wouldn't. Instead, you'd move heaven and earth to give it the breath of life it deserved. You'd find a way to bring current to the bulb, no matter the sacrifice, until it lit up the night. Why? Because at the nucleus of your existence is the desire to create (bulb) and to be part of all that is (current).

So then, just as you would offer your creation the right to connect to a current and fuel its purpose, Source holds in trust for you that same current until you're ready to accept the connection and believe you *deserve* to harness its limitless power. In a state of resistance to *what is* or that which you're born to express, you've essentially forgotten that you're an instrument of light. You live in darkness not because you want to, but because you're disconnected from the Source that gives you license to eradicate it.

The second theme, manifesting that which you're driven to express, requires you to move from *deserving* to *serving,* meaning you've accepted your right to the current and are now open to being in service, or lit up. You're willing to connect and practice harnessing the current that's been held in trust for, and *entrusted* to, you. To clarify, the term *service* in this instance is not akin to *servant.* Rather, it means to be in service to—and awakened by—your individual expression in any given moment and in life. In essence, you're plugged in and in flow with Source, Universal, and Grid current, thereby activating the Grid Work.

Like water, Grid current flows and creates a charged river that can carve a path through any terrain. Grid current is to water what rain is to parched earth: it gives life, nourishes and comingles to propagate the promise of creation. Seeing as your body is more than 60 percent water, current conduction is inevitable; the decision to bring into your awareness is *what* you choose to conduct: Source energy (Grid) or emotion (mind).

Energy and emotion are both currents and have the capacity to build in velocity, but they flow in opposing directions, as energy moves you *toward* that which you are born to express (in co-creation with Grid) and emotion moves you *away* from that which you are born to express (in co-creation with mind). Oftentimes, emotions are confused with feelings; however, they differ in that emotions are the mind's and ego's tools for keeping you separate (disconnected from the Grid) while feelings are heart-based, the antennae for the energetic current moving you toward that which you're born to express (connected to the Grid).

Let's look at a practical example. Ask a person what they *think* (mind / ego) about their overbearing boss, and you'll most likely receive an emotional response: "What a jerk. He's so controlling and irrational. He drives me insane." Within the grips of emotion, this person is completely disconnected from their conscious awareness; they are essentially asleep and being driven by the ego's need to defend, blame, and defame. The danger with being in this state is that this person is moving *away* from the current of whom they actually are; they are in resistance to *what is*, and therefore, misaligned with the—and their—truth.

Ask a person how they *feel* (heart) about their over-bearing boss, and you'll receive a deeper response: "He doesn't see the value I bring to the team. He doesn't allow me to use my talents. I'm suffocating." In touch with the heart, this person is in flow and moving with Grid current. They are consciously aware and not in a state of resistance to *what is*, which in this example is a boss who doesn't see or value them.

A person in touch with their feelings is a person connected to the Grid. Feelings are jellyfish-like tentacles that reach out and explore the world around them, then eventually lock onto the Source current fueling all that is. In this state, this person has access to their expression, and more importantly, their core authenticity. In our example, this person choosing feelings over emotions has brought a fundamental element into the equation: truth. This person's feelings (antennae to Grid current) have brought into their awareness the fact that they are in danger of moving out of flow—away from that which they are born to express.

Here's what they learn from their willingness to choose feelings instead of emotions: "He doesn't see the value I bring to the team" translates to "I'm valuable and deserve the opportunity to express" (to be in flow). "He doesn't allow me to use my talents" translates to "I know I'm talented and I desire the opportunity to embrace and shine my unique light" (to connect to the Grid energy and co-create). "I'm suffocating" translates to "I'm in darkness and I know, innately, I have the capacity to extricate myself" (harnessing the current of connection to illuminate that which is in darkness and flow).

What will happen now is a miracle in the making. With this person in acceptance of *what is* and aware of their truth, they will be in flow; as a result, they will resonate with the pulse of co-creation. Their signal, or energetic signature, will move from *I am what is done to me* to *I am what is made for me*—and what is made for them, for all of us, for *you*, is the very spark of creation.

In this magical co-creative space, fear cannot hold you. Suffering cannot suffocate you and resistance loses its power to drown you in stagnant waters. Buoyant and light-filled, you need only unleash the current of Universal flow, jump in, and ride the river wild.

RAFT NOT INCLUDED

Riding the river is a gloriously freeing experience, but it's not without its learning curve. You'll be bruised, bloodied, and water-choked along the way, but with every mile the river flows and with every minute you stay in its current-filled waters, you will get stronger and steadier.

Contrary to what most believe, water doesn't necessarily choose the path of least resistance. In truth, water's flow is at the mercy of both gravity and terrain. In this

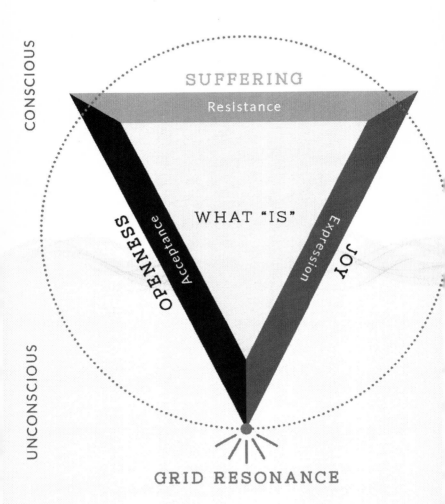

Unstuck

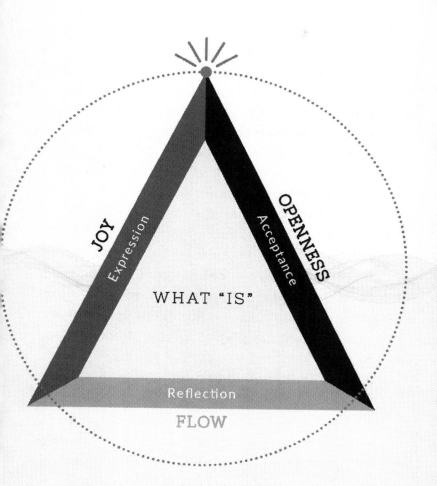

case, gravity is your soul's desire (purest expression) and terrain is your sole connection (relationship with self). Gravity, via a desire to express, *pulls* water toward it and works in conjunction with its flow. Terrain, via the status of the relationship with self, determines water's path and dictates its speed of flow, or depth of stagnation.

When we talk about relationship with self, it's important to set some parameters of understanding: *relationship with self* does not imply a mental construct, nor does it imply that nothing else matters. Relationship with self simply means, "I am aligned with the Grid, receiving Source flow and consistently bringing that which would cause suffering—to myself and others—into my conscious awareness."

This is not to be confused with being selfish, self-centered, or self-interested, which are states of being driven by the mind and ego ("I am my *own* Universe"). What's being outlined in relationship with self is driven and projected through Source ("I am a pillar *within* the Universe").

Further distilled, we have self-centeredness: "What *happen*s to me is my reality" translates to "defend and destroy." Versus, relationship with self: "My reality is what I *make* happen" translates to "comingle and co-create." In the latter instance, *self* can be defined as Source's and Grid's conduit for Universal expression. Ultimately, *you* are the vessel through which Source expresses creation and your unique inspiration turns that creation into that which you're born to express; the zenith of a co-creative Universal partnership and your path to joy.

Joy is a super signal that resonates outward—a frequency for transmitting, receiving, and attracting. Comparatively, suffering is also a frequency offering mirrored functions, but it differs in one critical aspect: suffering can only attract and transmit more suffering (static resonance), whereas joy can attract and transmit all that falls within its light-bearing signal (amplified resonance). Putting the concept into elemental form, we recognize that far more life can be sustained in clean flowing waters than can be in toxic stagnant waters.

Once you bring your resistance to *what is* into your consciousness awareness, you can move into reflection and, eventually, flow. Reflection allows you to float just outside the threshold of acceptance, giving you the opportunity to explore your passing resistance while working your way toward accepting the truth, or *what is*.

Reflection can be an incredibly useful state of being, as it fosters self-exploration and gives the unconscious mind permission to release information necessary to move you forward. Naturally, the unconscious is programmed to do this, but only in circumstances where it deems the environment safe and you stable enough to constructively process what's being released. Moreover, reflection shifts stagnancy into gentle flow while gradually washing away toxicity and bringing in freshly oxygenated water to nourish your soul.

With reflection having replaced resistance, your resonant signal rises in frequency and begins flirting with possibility and inspiration. These two channels are essential for expression and with even the smallest amount of the stardust they emit, you can defy gravity, reshape rugged terrain, and turn streams into rushing rivers.

HOW TO MOVE THE MOUNTAIN

Grid Focus: Self-assessment
Elemental Phase: I am but a mountain stream.

- Get still and breathe deeply until the sound of your own breathing is the only thing you hear—the only sound registering in your conscious mind. Once you're in this serene and quiet space, move to the next step.

- In your mind's eye, imagine a large white canvas in front of you. In your hand is a single paintbrush already loaded with paint. Keep breathing deeply, then thoughtfully ask your soul to paint the terrain and landscape surrounding it—the place where your soul resides. It's important not to engage the mind here, only the soul. The less you think, the better—just paint. Watch the canvas as the terrain and landscape take shape; stay focused on the freedom of painting versus what is *being* painted. Once your painting is complete, put the brush down and move to the next step.

- Study the terrain and landscape surrounding your soul. How do you *feel* when observing what's been painted? With your feelings as fuel, move into a state of reflection on where you are and what the painting is depicting. Once you are experiencing reflection, meaning there is no trace of resistance, move to the next step.

- Ask yourself (gently and without judgment): "Does the terrain and landscape surrounding me foster acceptance and joy?" Stay in the space of reflection and notice what comes into your awareness. There is some seeding going on here, as your unconscious will release information that will, if not now, eventually move you forward. Breathe deeply and hold the reflective space until you feel your body growing light and buoyant. Once you reach this physical state, it indicates your unconscious release is complete for this assessment (it will continue releasing more as the Grid Work goes deeper).

- Be kind and gentle with your body and heart after this exercise, and most importantly, drink plenty of water while repeating the silent mantra, "I am in flow with that which I am born to express."

CHAPTER THREE

The Deep End of the Ocean

WITH POSSIBILITY AND INSPIRATION now amplifying the resonance of your signal, you'll travel from the river of awakening to the ocean of divine exploration. Let's get clarity around the concept of *divine*. In this instance and for the purpose of this book, we are breaking the concept into two parts: *di*, meaning *twofold* or *double*, and *vine*, representative of a living, vein-like network from which fruit is yielded.

Twofold symbolizes your co-creative relationship with the Universe and once in union with that Force, you are *enfolded* into the richness of Universal flow. *Vine* speaks to the connectedness of all things, translating ultimately to the larger structure of the Grid.

The current that runs between the Grid and the oceanic Universal space in which you now float is the most powerful source you can access in human form. This electro-charged stream infuses you with a celestial spark while fostering growth and the shedding of encrusted soul-deadening debris; it is here that you will incubate your truest form of self.

Resistance, fear, self-hatred, and forced separation cannot survive in the nutrient-rich waters into which you're choosing to immerse, and you can now, in essence, experience a kind of synchronized swim with your soul. While you further detach from the mental framework of your resistance and become comfortable with *what is*, you will meet, allow, and *see* who you actually are—to the degree that you're able to let go and let flow.

If we snapshot your journey thus far, we have the awakening to *what is*, which triggers your state of resistance coming into your conscious awareness, in turn allowing your soul to resonate and communicate your truest expression.

As you flow toward the deeper end of your ocean, you will come into contact with all that you previously pushed downstream while in a state of resistance, an action driven by limitations placed on you by your mind and ego: "I'll follow that dream when I have enough money"; "I'll learn more about that interest when I'm not working so much"; "I'll spend more time on what

I love when my children/partner need me less"; "I'm happiest when I'm doing that hobby/pastime/activity, but I can't make money doing it. So why bother?"; or most commonly, "I'm happiest doing something I feel no one will respect/honor/understand."

In analyzing the thought patterns above, which are prevalent in all of us, you can see the circular pathways of self-neglect, stagnation, and confinement. Like a snake eating its own tail, our mind would have us subscribe to a belief system that causes our greatest asset—our soul-filled expression and corresponding connection to the Grid—to consume itself.

Such circular thinking makes us feel as though there is movement from one consideration to the next, but it's an illusion fashioned by the mind's need to secure what it deems a safe environment. In truth, this flurry of mental activity leads you back to where you started; only now, you're too exhausted to question your surroundings or the method used to entomb you within them.

It's important not to attack the mental construct and its respective function, as its efforts are in earnest and driven by age-old assumptions derived from our primitive roots. The impulses of the mind will not cease with this Grid Work, nor will they ease their assault, but they will have to pass through a newly adopted filter: your conscious awareness, or willingness to accept *what is*.

By moving through this purifying net of accepting *what is*, you will clearly see *what is not*—or that which is out of alignment with your soul and its truest expression—and in allowing that truth to enter into your conscious awareness, the mind loses its power. Now when it releases its circular thought patterns, you'll have a different relationship to both what you're experiencing and what your mind is choosing to show you because you are not bound by resistance or fear; you are willing and able to identify *what is* and therefore able to create in resonance with your expression.

Playing this out in metaphor, as with Dorothy in Oz, you'll have the ability to pull back the curtain and see the truth of the self-proclaimed Wizard (mind), which is that he only projects a portion of the truth, a curated version of himself and his environment (mental construct). Fast-forwarding to the story's end, once Dorothy has taken in the full journey and associated information, she realizes everything she needs is already within her: she is her own wizard and her own source of magic.

So, when the tornado of the mind whips up and carries you away to a strange and unknown land filled with circular paths and story-based characters, you need only call upon the truth of your soul—your ruby slippers—to safely carry you back home, or back to your natural, resting state of balance. When heart, soul, and spirit are aligned with the Grid's current, you are in a perpetual state of harmonic resonance, where you radiate what you desire to receive and you receive what you intend to create.

Let's look at a practical example: Sally has a job/ profession/role that sustains her just enough to keep her on the circular path of the mental plane. Yet something deep inside—her true expression—pushes upward and every so often, pounds on the door of her consciousness with fists of longing, sadness, and discontentment.

Sally may entertain the idea of opening the door for a few seconds before she is struck down by mental resistance: "You are lucky to have a job in this economic climate"; "Think of all the people who can't pay their bills"; "You don't have a skillset to get something better, and there are people with more advanced degrees"; "Other women would kill to have a partner like yours"; "You can't switch careers now—you'd lose everything you've worked for"; and so on.

Sally has now eaten her own tail and has let the mind stop her from pulling back the curtain and finding the wizard—the magic—within her. Instead, she muddles her way through knowing her heart longs for something more meaningful, her very soul using its resounding voice to demand its right to create, to express. But her state of resistance deadens her instincts and the resulting forced circular motion perpetuates Sally's refusal to accept *what is*, which in this case is her disconnection from her expression.

In one way or another, we can all identify with Sally's plight. Again, it's your *relationship* with your plight that matters. And the first step to unearthing your purest expression is to accept *what is*. The moment you bring your truth into your conscious awareness and allow it to permeate your alchemical experience, you have exited the mental plane and merged with the co-creative current of the Grid.

In acknowledging that you're not aligned with that which you are born to express, you have moved away from a state of resistance and into a state of discovery. *Di-vine* exploration is now part of your elemental DNA, and it will infuse you with the light of possibility and creative play. By doing this, in many ways, you have conquered the hardest part of this work, which is to leave the mental plane of resistance and leap into the ocean of the unknown—a body of liquid magic teaming with limitless life.

You were not born to suffer. You were not born to suppress your spark. You were not born to live only half your truth. Everyone has a unique signature of light that is theirs alone, their guiding star above a dark sea. It doesn't matter where you came from, what's been done to you, or how many people made you believe you weren't born to run, to fly—what matters is that you leap. That's all it takes to start the awakening. You don't have to do anything else at this point. You're enough just as you are, floating in the unknown and soaking up the majesty of your making. You are precious, you matter, and you are not alone.

GO FISH

There's a vast difference between floating in the freedom of the limitless unknown and floating, yet stagnating, in the discontented known. It's an important distinction to understand that water *known* isn't always water *stagnant*. Still waters of the known—when in alignment with the Grid—can allow for an open-channeled current to growth and joy.

While floating in the newness of your acceptance of *what is*, you now have the capacity to do something that in putrid, motionless waters you wouldn't dare: turn and float belly-down, face submerged with your eyes open, staring into the ocean of who you are. Breathing is effortless as, like an unborn child, you rely on the current-filled cord between your ocean and the Grid to serve as your lifeline; a cord that is infused with the elemental strands you need to grow.

Having rotated *in to*, rather than floating *on top of*, the ocean of yourself, you have moved from acceptance to surrender. This is where your elemental evolution begins. Here, you will see all that makes up, lives within, and relies upon your oceanic environment to survive; you can observe the entire ecosystem on which your being is based.

This is why the first stage of the Grid Work, the Sounding, is paired with water: it's the element that allows for surrender, incubation, saturation, and exploration. Only the ocean of *you* can offer the insights needed to surrender to the unknown, eventually flowing you from *what is* to *what's next*.

As with the planetary ocean, nothing within your oceanic ecosystem operates without connection to itself: what dies gives life, what changes forces adaptation, what gets consumed is transformed, then dispersed and repurposed. The system is cyclical and most importantly, circular. Your ocean contains all that you are, all that has happened to you, all that you come from, and all that you will become—each respective event leading back into the broader ecosystem.

This is evidenced by countless change-makers throughout history, each with their own stories of adversity, pain, and insurmountable obstacles. Yet the common current running between them is their ability to allow their ecosystems to work for them, on their behalf and for their benefit. Oftentimes, those who radiate the brightest lights are those who came from the darkest of circumstances; they used the influence of darker matter to seek the resonance of their innate light, which is the essence of the ecosystem in play.

As a non-parallel example, imagine a large ship sinking and taking with it a cargo of valuable imported goods. For the shipping company, the loss is devastating but results in the implementation of improved safety regulations for ships and their crews. For the manufacturer of the goods, the loss triggers an executive to invent a shipping container with an emergency raft inflation mechanism, which becomes a shipping standard, in turn saving millions of dollars in lost goods. The vessel itself transforms into a haven for sea life, a steely coral reef that positively affects the environment in which it's submerged.

Clearly, this scenario cannot be form-fitted to the events in a human life, but the nature of cause and effect, necessity to invention, and dark to light can be extracted and applied. For it's the willingness to step out of resistance, move into acceptance, then flow into surrender that allows the scenario's participants to thrive. What's being illustrated is that each scenario's participant is willing to float in an ocean of possibility, then take the spark of creation and forge a way forward.

With that in mind, studying the inhabitants of your life-filled sea will provide invaluable insight. You'll see all the colors, creatures, and mysteries existing in the deep end of your ocean. And there, too, will be sharks and dark-finned giants emerging from the shadows to get a better look at you. Rest assured, nothing you'll see is to be feared, as these things, both beautiful and beastly, are part of you. They have always been there, and they always will be. It's your relationship to them—and how you use it in tandem with the spark of creation—that will change.

As you marvel at the inhabitants of your ocean and surrender to the experience, know that what has happened to you informs *what* you are, but not *who* you are. The *what* is a label, the *who* is eternal. You are what you're born to express, as that is the pinnacle of your light. Therefore, any labels forced upon you are external, whereas you are *eternal*.

Your ocean is a body of water: it lives, it breathes, it feels, and it's renewing and flowing with resilience and bounty. So, harness the curiosity that fuels *di-vine* exploration and dive. Swim strong, go deep, and revel in the richness of all that makes you, you.

HOW TO MOVE THE MOUNTAIN

Grid Focus: Self-assessment
Elemental Phase: I am but an ocean, deep.

- Get still and imagine the air around you transforming into water. See yourself submerged, yet breathing easily: air and water are now one.

- Drink in several long, slow breaths and feel the sensation of water and air having merged. Focus on how it feels on your tongue, in your throat, and in your lungs. Notice how calming the sensation is, as though you are one with the liquid air and energized by the richness it offers.

- Play with these sensations in your mind, being able to stay underwater endlessly. Breathing effortlessly.

- Now imagine that your pores are emitting a light-gray substance, almost as though liquid clouds are escaping from your skin. As you watch the cloudy vapor gently leak from your skin and begin floating around you, notice how light you feel. How free.

- Take your time watching the gray cloud-like vapor ebb and flow in the gently rocking current. You're breathing without effort, one with water and air, and peacefully taking in your environment.

- Without urging from you, notice how the gray vapor mutes to white, then eventually becomes transparent until you can no longer decipher the vapor leaving your pores from the surrounding water.

- Experience every moment that passes as blissful; you are lighter, clearer, and increasingly more comfortable breathing the liquid air continuing to move in and out of your lungs.
- Stay with the feeling of releasing and breathing as long as possible. Then, when you're ready, watch the water around you transform into pure air. As though having evaporated into a warm breeze, the water becomes completely replaced by air. Stay with the visualization of being calm, dry, and unburdened.

The Void

ELEMENT: **AIR**

"O, wind, if winter comes,
can spring be far behind?"
—PERCY BYSSHE SHELLEY

CHAPTER FOUR

Basecamp

UPON ENTERING THE SECOND STAGE, the Void, which is paired with air, we leave our oceanic exploration and begin forging a path from the base of our mountains upward. The word *void* is deceiving, as we've been taught that it's a state of being without, or a scenario in which there is nothing where there should, in fact, be something. In truth, the Void can be a purifying and fulfilling sensation to experience.

The Void we're examining exists because you've moved from accepting and surrendering to *what is*, and now desire to drift into *what's next*. Allowing the truth of what isn't aligned with your true expression to enter your conscious awareness clears the channel for its eventual passing: what is out of resonance drops from your frequency, while what *is* in resonance aligns with your signal of expression.

The space and time required for your frequency to retune are, in essence, the Void. There is a fine distinction in how this instrumental period can be viewed, as the silence and emptiness you feel is not nothingness or dead air, but rather, it's your soul finally being allowed to breathe, to seek. The current of your being is now vibrating with possibility while forming its unique signature, leading to the eventual state of radiating soul-filled sound. This sound wave is supported by the cloud-like platform of your intention to purely express, then amplified by your connection to the Grid.

In truth, the Void is one of the most honest states in which you'll find yourself because you've accepted *what is*, surrendered to seeking, and ceased the mind's incessant insistence that you are anything other than your truest expression. In a way, there is release in the Void. You can rest here in the tent of your surrender, at the base of the mountains formed by your spirited soul and listen to the gentle wind. You are free in this space. There is no pressure to be anything other than who you truly are.

While the Void is a horizontal plane, the refining of your frequency is a vertical plane, or rather, a path. The journey, or Walk, up the mountain takes patience, steadiness, and scrutiny, seeing as you will be creating the path as you move, step-by-step, moment by moment.

The focus it takes to measure and calculate each foot-
hold is a critical aspect of the Walk because it requires
you to be in the present: you cannot walk forward if you
are looking backward.

Staying true to the present as you begin your Walk
gives your soul time for recreation and your mind space
for reformation. Whereas your previous exploration in
the ocean of you provided insight into the ecosystem
that makes up your operating constitution, or how you
view and absorb the world around you, the journey up
the mountain will reveal the secrets and whispers of
your spirit. By beginning this Walk, you will bear wit-
ness to the whispers of your spirit and in tandem with
the release of its once-silenced voice, your spirit will
start the process of unlocking your psyche.

It's important to understand that the work outlined
in this book is not a replacement for psychological care.
In fact, psychological exploration with a psychotherapeutic professional, in conjunction with this work, is
highly recommended. The mention of the psyche in the
context of the Grid Work pertains to the spirit aspects
of the psyche that act as influencers, versus the physical and environmental aspects of your life experiences
that may have affected psychological structure. Distilled
further, the Grid Work is current-based (energetic) and
psychotherapeutic work is body-based (mechanic).

Take note that the mind is not associated with this
chapter's psychological exploration; rather, it's the

body's intelligence we're seeking to incubate and soul resonance for which we're fostering growth: "Body knows mind's foes and spirit flows where soul-current goes." Meaning, body and soul meet at the intersection of intuition—which is not a mental function—and once developed can become your innermost source of internal governing. Higher wisdom and self-parenting are the ultimate forms of release from the confines of the mind's suffocating hold, and traveling along the path of your mountain will ignite this glorious process.

When we're born, we understand that we are magical. We comprehend our own power and innately know that we're formed from the genesis of light, our souls forged from light's very Source. Therefore, we are not humans seeking to experience light; we *are light* experiencing being human.

Between environmental influences, emotional misalignments, and physical experiences, we forget who we are. Our light dims not because it's in danger of being extinguished, but rather, because we've forgotten how to reignite and fuel its flame. One of the most fundamental elements of light or fire is air: oxygen is to flame what awakening is to light. What we're seeking is not to *find* ourselves, but instead to *remember* ourselves and reignite the eternal flame of our expression.

Elemental alignment, the act of activating and balancing the elements within us, is the key to awakening. This alignment begins as an ignition point, and it can manifest subtly as a deep longing, a feeling of purposelessness, or it can occur as a more dramatic, catalyst-causing life event. Regardless of how the ignition point is activated, you will awaken and begin the process of elemental alignment.

Prior to the ignition point, there is a prestate or precursory stage known as the divide. This stage is usually marked by a feeling that something is missing, that *you* are missing. The divide sends gentle pings toward your soul, until like a bloodless heart, it regains its flow and starts to beat. With the pulse of your soul sending its rhythm to your spirit, you will resonate the frequency of awakening until you eventually draw the ignition point experience into your life.

However, the state, or stage you are currently in, is far less vital than your willingness to *be* in it—to explore. The combined wisdom of your spirit and soul knows how to support you on this journey. They were created to bring you back to the light and to guide you toward remembering your magnificence.

Spoken plainly, you are a magician. Highly skilled, arcane in your knowledge, and utterly unique in your expression, you are capable of creating and casting light because it's from light that you are made.

BABY STEP

At the base of your mountain, it is spring. Flowers bloom, streams run free, animals flit across your path, and nature's bounty is evident in every direction. You are poised to begin your Walk and take the first inaugural step up the steep incline of your chosen mountain.

First, breathe. Then, elect to align with the life-sustaining element of air. Feel it in your lungs, cells, blood, and heart. Sense the rhythm of your spirit and know that your frequency is in the process of retuning. Pure embodiment of air brings with it a feeling of lightness, freedom, and resilience.

In order to move closer to what's next, you need to open your consciousness to *otherness*. Broken down, *otherness* means that you're aware of what's not aligned, seeking what's next, and joyful about the possibility of what can be. Aligning with the elemental properties of air means there are no boundaries, confines, or edges to what you can illuminate, intend, or imagine.

It's important to note that *imagine* is not the same as *dream*. The basis for imagining is the soul's resonance transmuting physical and mental barriers while projecting into your consciousness and onto your mind's eye. Dreaming is a powerful tool for the initial stages of awakening as it triggers the creative spark; but once on the elemental path, it can serve as a confining force to that which you are born to express. Essentially, imagining opens a tri-channel between heart, spirit, and soul *without* mental judgment as to the direction of motion, whereas dreaming opens a dual-channel between mind and body *with* mental judgment as to the direction of motion.

For example, if an individual is always dreaming of being a singer, they will shape their world around that dream, often ignoring surfacing talents and soul signs (otherness) that would otherwise move them toward their truest expression, which may or may not entail being a singer. Their frequency's message is dangerously rigid and effectively, their dream has narrowed the path of possibility.

If that same individual shifts into imagining, they will widen their path and raise their frequency by radiating a similar, yet crucially adjusted message that allows for the soul's expression to inform their frequency and subsequent resonance. The inelastic demand of the dreamer—"I am a singer"—may not leave room for their truest expression, which might be, "I am a songwriter." In this illustration, the individual's truest and most powerful form of expression, their tri-channel of joy, is songwriting, singing, *and* the business of selling their songs. If they keep an iron hold on the original structure of their dream, they may miss a more fulfilling, lucrative, and truer form of expression. Therefore, imagining is expansive and led by the expression, whereas dreaming is contractive and subject to the mental plane.

Being in a state of otherness while using the expansiveness of imagining is what will lead you to what's next and, eventually, that which you are born to express. As you take your first few steps up the mountain, notice how the path forms *as* you walk, *because* you walk. The cause and effect of your step forming the path brings to light the structure of your co-creative relationship with the Grid.

When you send out a soul pulse of openness to move toward your truest expression, the Universal Force will respond in kind and that comingling of openness meeting Force creates a space of pure possibility. If, when sending that soul pulse, you are aligned with otherness and open to the truth of your expression, you will amass an atomic powered beam of light that charges your spirit and propels you into the realm of what's next.

As with your oceanic exploration, your path will not always be rose-lined, rainbow-adorned, or filled with fluffy bunnies. It's plausible, and likely, that when dusk falls, you will encounter the things that go bump in the night, creatures in the shadows, and beasts you've starved prior to awakening. Take heart and know that nothing you encounter can harm you: your psyche and soul will not release anything you cannot handle or understand. That is Universal law, and it is unbending.

Everything within you is of Source-light creation. Meaning, the characters you meet on this journey, the knowledge that surfaces, and the remembrances coming into your consciousness form a tapestry woven with light-bearing thread. Within your exploration, you *are* safe. Staying in your otherness and expanding into your Walk requires a deep level of vulnerability. It's natural to feel a slight contraction around that concept.

When aligning with new elements and breaking free of the mind's grasp, you will have periodic mini-quakes, which are simply the mind and ego reminding you that they're there. What's important is to honor their need to be seen without judgment while gently telling them that you are committed to *di-vine* exploration, elemental alignment, and living in true expression. Calmly, peacefully, you can let them know that they are seen, but only through the rearview mirror.

Open your heart and take the next series of steps knowing that you are protected, courageous, and light-filled. Explore your surroundings and marvel at your mountain. See the flowers you've planted, growing tall and wild. Stand in awe of the seedlings you've tended, which are now leafy giants, then take in the perfumed air of all the sweetness inside you.

This is what it means to meet your spirit and when you do, you'll fundamentally alter your relationship with you. It changes you at your very core and when you begin to remember who you are, when you take the first steps into the warmth of your own light, it alters your chemical structure at a cellular level, in turn making you alchemical. When you not only comprehend—but *feel*—that you are born to climb, you will call the wind and let it guide your ascent.

HOW TO MOVE THE MOUNTAIN

Grid Focus: Self-assessment
Elemental Phase: I am but a breath of air.

- Imagine you are at the base of a beautiful mountain range. Spring is in full bloom, the air is crisp, and a gentle breeze drifts past you, carrying with it the scent of pine and wildflowers.
- You are in the most peaceful surroundings you've ever experienced. You are innately aware that nothing can harm you here; you are completely protected and safe. Breathe in the feeling of safety as though it's life-giving, oxygenated air.
- Focus to the left of you and notice the color of the grass, the wildflowers. See everything nature has to offer in this moment. Take your time and let your mind play with the details as though creating a living painting. The more vivid and specific the details, the better.
- Now, focus to the right and notice the bank of trees in the distance. See the breeze rustling the leaves, allowing sunlight to peek through and send shadowed reflections toward the fertile ground. Allow your mind and spirit to be uninhibited in your imaginings; create whatever moves and delights you.
- Once you're fully immersed in the landscape to your right and left, look in front of you and see only white

space—as though you are creating the world around you at your will. In this assessment, you see what you have imagined to your right and left but understand that what is in front of you is not yet created. As a result, you see only cloud-filled space, beautiful in its simplicity and emptiness.

- As you look out into the soft white clouds, feel your spirit fill with excitement knowing you can create whatever you desire. The path you will create, the mountain you will ascend, is forming *as* you walk, with you and most importantly, *for* you.

- When you're completely comfortable with the empty, cottony space in front of you, finding the clouds and white space serene, take a breath and take a single step. As you step down, notice a path beginning to form beneath your foot just as it touches the ground.

- Remember, you are forming the path *one step at a time*. All you see is the path beneath your foot. There is no landscape to speak of, the horizon only that of white cottony space. Be with the sensation of watching in wonder while you create the terrain as you walk, and most importantly, as you like.

- Rejoice in the sense of play while taking a second step; take your time and imagine the path's details clearly. Experience how the path feels beneath your foot, whether it be soft earth, rocky terrain, or grass—see it and *sense* it. Then, take another step.

CHAPTER FIVE

Pathfinder

PRESENCE OF MIND IS CRUCIAL when beginning the Walk, with each step being informed by your whole being—*being* in the moment. If this concept is processed mathematically, we could say: $1 + 1 = 2$ and that within this equation, we know the ones (1s) are neither wondering what they were or what they will be, nor are they anxious to be something other than ones (1s). In the moment, they are simply ones (1s) and in their willingness to be part of something larger than themselves—which is to become the additive form of two (2)—they have surrendered to *what is* and unleashed the Law of Possibility.

Translated to the Walk, it's important to understand that the path will only form to the toe-edge of the foot you just put down: meaning, the path is created as you walk, *because* you walk. Therefore, the only moment that exists is the structure of $1 + 1 = 2$, or *co-creation + being = manifestation in motion toward your truest expression*. That is the present moment at its purest: the co-creative Universe, you and your *being*, and the path you're manifesting toward your truest expression.

Were you to look back, you would find only pathless terrain. Were you to look forward, the result would be the same. For instance, within our example, if the ones (1s) looked back, they would become zeroes (0s). If they looked forward, they would destabilize the structure of the equation *co-creation + being = manifestation in motion toward their truest expression*, and instead clumsily crash manifestation and expression into one another, resulting in an outcome distorted from their original intention.

Practically applied, focusing on the past (going from one [1] to zero [0]) causes you to leave co-creative Universal space. Focusing on, or worrying about, the future takes you out of a state of *being*, or a state of Universal flow. In essence, when not in the present moment, you cannot, in any way, accurately manifest that which you are uniquely designed to express.

There is only one reason your mind urges you to look either behind or ahead of you: fear. And with an arsenal of panic-inducing weapons, fear often catapults you into the lands of *if only* and *what if*. Then, trapped on foreign soil with only one path offering two narrow directions: "If only I'd done things differently," and "What if I make the same mistake?" you are too paralyzed to create in the present moment. You are stuck.

But you needn't stay stuck and can instead acknowledge that fear is a byproduct of the primitive mind. Your experience can shift from resisting fear and what it's showing you to accepting *what is*, which is that you are—temporarily—under the mind's control. Once you accept *what is*, you are immediately released from fear's grasp and realigned with the present moment.

The mind's stronghold is pervasive because it's been in charge and at the helm of our experience throughout our evolutionary process. Fear is a tool it uses to exert the control it *thinks* is necessary to help you survive, to keep you alive. Letting that concept sink in is important, as vilifying the mind and working against it puts you back into a state of resistance.

In order to accept *what is* and flow, it's necessary to respect that the mind is seeking to honor its commitment to take care of you—to save you. Once you embrace that the mind is a glorious part of you that wants to partner *with* you, you can shift and craft your relationship with it in a way that serves your greater path-forging journey.

In staying present and walking your path, you will retrain the mind and instill within it a new code of conduct—a retooled way to serve its purpose. With each step, the mind will learn that you're safest while in flow with the present moment because it is there that the spark of creation—the purest form of light—resides. Once it comprehends the difference between existing within light (creation) and existing within fear (darkness), it will recalibrate and begin working in tandem with your intuition to help you immerse in the present moment.

Learning to align with the present moment is transformative in that it takes you from being chemical (artificially purified and produced) to alchemical (a magic process of creation). And, lest we enter into undefined territory, in the context of the Grid Work, *Magic* simply means Matter And Grid In Co-creation.

Materialized matter when aligned with the Universal Grid can transcend the laws of nature by co-creating a *super-nature, al-chemical* environment, or *super-nature-al[chemical]* existence. Once we commit to and begin the Walk, our very nature and material makeup becomes *supernatural*, which in turn calls all of our components— heart, mind, soul, and body—into alignment so we can create at a *magic-al[chemical]* level.

Distilled to its base, this concept can be paralleled to the process by which a diamond is formed. Whereby under the intense pressure of gravity and exposure to the heat of the earth's core, one type of matter transforms into another—carbon atoms organizing to form a crystalline structure. It's purely scientific, yet seemingly magical. It's both tangible and awe-inspiring, as is our own transformative process and resulting prismatic, diamond-dusted spirit.

We were designed to generate and radiate light, but before we learn to harness our supernatural magic, we must first pass through the gates of gravity and heat. There is a threshold just beyond those gates where your Walk begins, where you pick up your beloved companions—your heart and soul—and as one, make your way up the mountain.

CLOUD NINE

When we inhale deeply, our lungs expand to accommodate the incoming air. Conversely, when we exhale, our lungs contract in order to foster a process of exchange: carbon-heavy air for oxygen-rich air. Systemically, our bodies understand that expansion, contraction, and the resulting exchange are vital to our survival. In parallel, our souls and hearts go through a similar, if not far deeper, interchange.

Continuing your Walk and staying present forms a path toward your expression while allowing your heart to exhale and your soul to inhale. Just as our lungs clarify and refine the air we breathe, the relationship between our heart and soul is filtered through the spirit. Within the stage of the Void, the spirit does some of its most profound work purifying, then circulating the Universal light-infused air we need to contract then expand into our truest form of expression.

From a Universal perspective, the spirit is air's counterpart and without it, the heart and soul cannot breathe. The heart pumps and circulates our body's blood, but it's also the origination point of our resonant energetic frequency. As the heart pumps, it creates a rhythm and that rhythm radiates outward, creating a Universal pulse. That pulse is retuned and clarified by the spirit before being amplified by the soul.

Each of these points of contact between the heart, spirit, and soul forms a kind of umbilical cord that connects us to the Grid, which is how we plug in to receive inspiration, to recharge, or to unburden. Forming your path one step at a time allows your heart, soul, and spirit to purify their divine connection. For your frequency is only as clear as your heart, soul, and spirit are pure.

Therefore, the *speed* of your ascent matters. Slow, steady steps allow your physical and spirit-based counterparts to reset and purify. The Walk isn't a race but rather an alchemical transformation, and it needs you in the present moment and committed to the interchange taking place between your heart and soul via the spirit.

As you make your way up the mountain, the air will thin while dense clouds begin to appear. The air thins as the spirit fosters a more efficient connection between heart and soul, and clouds form as the atmosphere begins absorbing the debris released from the spirit's purification process.

The higher you ascend, the thicker the cottony white clouds will become until your path is scarcely visible. It's just you, the gently whistling wind, and the rhythmic pulse of your heart. With the mind focused on your journey and your spirit unburdening your heart and soul, you can tap into true, unadulterated joy.

Joy is the frequency of the soul, the conduit of the spirit, and without it, you suffocate your connection to the light. Resonating with a signal of joy frees the heart from the daily trials we place upon it. And because our hearts are connected to the spirit and soul, they foster an infallible form of body intelligence, where, in truth, there is nothing our bodies don't know. They know when we're in danger, they know when someone or something isn't safe, they know when we're unwell, they know when we're overtaxed, they know when we're truly in love, and they know when we're not.

Our bodies are the heart's mouthpiece—they are how the heart and its light-filled connection participates in and understands the human experience. When in a state of joy, you reset the link between the body and the heart. You quite literally reboot the software back to factory settings, which are those of full Source alignment.

With the heart unweighted and wrapped in the frequency of joy, your body can begin communicating the heart's messages, in turn sharpening your intuition and leading you closer to that which you are born to express. The levers we press and pull to manipulate our hearts, and ultimately our bodies, are equalized when in a state of joy, and it is here that we can begin to move from *what is* to *what's next.*

True joy can only be experienced while in the present moment and in total alignment (acceptance) with *what is*. Part of the clarity joy brings is in helping us see where we betray ourselves through false promises and self-manipulation: "I'll take a break when I get my promotion"; "I'll date when I lose ten pounds"; "I'll treat myself to a nice dinner after I've saved enough to buy my house/apartment. Until then, it's Top Ramen and Lean Cuisine."

We betray and manipulate ourselves because we're avoiding the cry of the heart, the ping of the spirit, and the reverberating shockwave of the soul to stop and accept the invitation to move toward our truest expression—toward our bliss. In this, we rob ourselves of our own humanity by subverting the very reason we *are* human, which is for our light to co-create and express.

Oftentimes, we use our hearts as an engine for consumption: "This/that is my heart's desire"; "I love him/her with all my heart"; "You/that broke my heart"; and so on. These are ego-serving statements and concepts that have hijacked the heart's identity in order to consume. Just as the mind believes controlling you with fear will keep you safe, the ego believes consuming will keep you safe—that the more you are/have/do/become, the bigger and more secure you are. However, as the mind recalibrates on the Walk, your ego will also learn that safety lies in learning to subsume versus consume.

To subsume entails including one thing in something else, whereas to consume entails using up or absorbing all surrounding attention or energy. With the purification process being fostered by the spirit, the heart and ego will shift the dynamics of their relationship. As a result, the ego will learn that you are safest when that which you truly intend is aligned with that which you are born to express.

For example, an ego impulse may be, "My heart's desire is to get/have that person," but in truth, the heart's signal doesn't function in this manner. It doesn't seek to control, dominate, or seduce. A message driven by the heart without the ego's interference would be, "I intend to share my life with a partner who sees and values me." The heart's message resonates on a completely different frequency than the ego's, as it's working in tandem with the spirit and soul; therefore, the heart's true intention is part of something else, or subsumed under and *in* to the soul's greater directive.

The ego, as with the mind, is archaic in how it views its role. It believes keeping you safe requires being in a constant state of consuming what's in its path. Akin to a cocker spaniel believing it's safer as a grizzle bear, the ego consumes all the things it believes will make it a grizzly bear. But it cannot become a bear through the channels of consumption; it can only change through the transformative nature of subsumption: by absorbing itself into something greater than it is—the dog doesn't become *the* bear; it becomes *part* of the bear. That something greater is Source and its invitation for you to align with that which you are born to express.

The ego has deceived you into living life with a hungry heart, a fervent desire to consume, love, feel, move, and act. Again, the ego is only doing what it believes is best to keep you safe until such a time as it recalibrates and recognizes a new way to carry out its mission. What's important to understand is that your heart is not hungry and in a balanced state, it does not desire to consume. Rather, your heart is full and innately connected to Universal law, which states: "All things aligned with the expression of light can only receive light."

Does it mean you won't ever have a bad day? No. Does it mean you won't feel the pains of alignment and growth? It doesn't. But it does mean you will come to know a deeper form of peace as you flow through your lessons. It does mean you are never alone, without or unguided. And, most importantly, it does mean you can alchemically alter your circumstances with efficiency and grace.

Your entire being is designed to play within the infinite space of co-creative possibility. At your disposal are the supernatural gifts given to you for the sole purpose of manifesting your joy, your soul's path, and your true expression. Magic does exist, and it starts at your fingertips and travels down to the tips of your toes until step-by-step, you create a path to the light—*your* light.

So, walk steady and walk true. Let your radiant light be a lamp unto your feet.

HOW TO MOVE THE MOUNTAIN

Grid Focus: Self-assessment
Elemental Phase: I am but a weightless cloud.

- Imagine yourself walking along a beautiful mountain path that magically forms beneath your feet as you take each step. See the path appear as your foot comes down and marvel at the co-creative relationship you have with your environment.

- Breathe deeply and take in the mountain air as you walk slowly, one step at a time, cognizant of the bounty of the moment. Notice how full you feel: full of oxygen, full of life, full of possibility.

- With each step, allow your burdens to lift. You need not identify them, see them, or even comprehend what they are; just stay with the intention to unburden. Understand that where you are going, no burdens can follow.

- Let your mind's eye fill with cottony white clouds that feel soft as they brush against your skin. Enjoy the sensation of their presence as though they're there to play with you, lift you, and lighten your burden.

- Allow the clouds to surround you, cushion you, and move with you. Feel as though your feet scarcely touch the ground until you realize the clouds are guiding you. Stay with the sensation of white cloudy space and notice how safe and weightless you feel.

- Let your mind become cloud-like as it merges into the surrounding cottony space. Allow yourself to enter a state of deep and thorough trust: you and the clouds are one. You are completely at peace while in motion with them, your only thoughts being those of oneness with the air around you.
- Let your body become so enmeshed with the air and clouds that you feel you are made of air. Give your creativity and imagination permission to play as you merge into, and become, sweet mountain air.
- Know with every particle of your being that you are without burden. You are a gentle breeze. You are a whisper in the wind. You are a light-infused current taking flight.

CHAPTER SIX

Windbreaker

AS YOU MAKE YOUR WAY up the mountain, you will begin aligning with the Law of Potentiality, which will further accelerate your unburdening while bringing you closer to that which you are born to express. Such rapid releasing is invigorating, but it's not without its challenges. Namely, learning to harness the winds of change rather than feeling they'll sweep you away from your newly forged path.

The density you once possessed is dissipating, which leaves you temporarily uprooted. With the ego and mind being retooled and retrained, they will have lifted their false, rigid roots from the ground while realigning with their soul-directed function. It's during this time that you may feel as though the air whipping up and around you is destabilizing your sense of identity and place in the world. Yet, rest assured that what's occurring is precisely the opposite.

The Law of Potentiality is built upon two main pillars: affinity and *pre*ceptive ability. Most of us are out of alignment with the Law of Potentiality because we have confused identity with affinity, and the act of being perceptive with the art of being *pre*ceptive.

Examining the first pillar, *affinity*, and taking the concept down to its base requires us to establish that we don't actually have an identity. At least not in the way our ego would have us believe. We are not what we do, how we look, or what we have. Identity, as related to the humanistic profile, doesn't actually exist. You can think of it like being in a room filled with beautiful furniture, but were you to put pressure on the pieces in any way, they would crumble beneath your weight as though made of papier-mâché.

Oftentimes, we focus on the details of the furniture, perfecting its outward appearance to the detriment of all else until we believe the pieces with their velvet and silk fabrics—their seemingly perfect structure—are real. The truth is that our identities, just like the papier-mâché furniture, are fabricated and cannot in any way hold the quantum mass of our true expression.

Your heart, soul, and spirit know this to be the case, which is why they quietly call to you from the background of your consciousness. Their chorus is one of unification and a longing to be closer to the light, which is most likely being smothered by the false structures you've created, for beneath those manufactured structures is the nucleus of *you*. And that electric pulse of energy and illuminating light are far more sacred, stable, and secure than any of the falsified identities you've constructed.

Rather than an identity, what we do possess is a unique frequency that radiates its own resonant signature. No one has been born with your talent, no one can edge you out of that which you are born to express, and no one can take away the undiluted power of your light-bearing signal. You are created from light with the sole purpose of expressing your specific frequency, and the purity of that tonal note is propelled outward to join the greater chorus of Source's expansive Grid.

Therefore, you are not a separate note playing alone in empty space; rather, you are resonating as part of a complex, multilayered symphony. All of us are instruments of light and must do our part to fine-tune the Grid's most important orchestral work: Universal balance. That is where we're heading and the more of us aligned with that which we are born to express, the more thoroughly we can participate in lighting up the Grid, which is the structure of all that is and all that will be.

A contrasting concept to identity, *affinity* is the first pillar of the Law of Potentiality, which aligns light with light. Affinity is our soul and spirit in kinship with the

Grid; it is one light structure recognizing the divinity in another. Affinity tethers us to the one Universal truth: "That which is made of light must express light."

Were we to pull in the earlier example, we would see that creating an identity is a mental construct designed to manufacture what we deem a safe and controlled environment. That environment is carefully curated and constantly tended to ensure the paint is always fresh, the fabric without blemish, and even if the pieces being upholstered cannot hold weight, it's how they *appear* that drives the identity-building impulse. It's born of the false mental assumption: "All that appears stable will eventually *become* stable," which results in suffering and the destabilization of joy.

What's being left out in this false-building scenario is the greater opportunity for co-creation. When working with affinity, we create on a grander scale: the builder goes from using papier-mâché and fabric to creating with the alchemical materials of the Universe. In essence, when working with identity, we are merely builders using limited resources. When working with affinity—connected to the larger Source from which we're formed—we become supernatural[chemical] architects using limitless resources. And in this, we find the resulting structure stable, secure, and most importantly, able to support the quantum mass of light that embodies our true expression.

The second pillar of the Law of Potentiality centers on the art of being *pre*ceptive rather than the act of being perceptive. As convincing as it seems, what we perceive in any given situation or environment is not reality. Through the filters of the ego, mind, and the opinions of others, we have distorted the process by which we *internalize* external information and apply it to our experience. Meaning, by the time we're in the process of perceiving, we have already passed the opportunity to originate from a Grid-aligned state.

In being *preceptive*, we allow the spirit and soul to *externalize* internal information; thereby, taking information out of the hands of mind and ego and processing it through a higher frequency that is tonally aligned with the Grid. Based upon word origins, *precept* equates to instruct before taking, whereas *percept* equates to seize or understand. Simply viewing these Latin origins (forgoing modern interpretation and usage) gives you the energetic signature of both states while clearly illustrating that one is in flow, while the other is forced and manufactured.

As an example, let's say you're on a bicycle intensely focusing on what's in front of you, when another cycler cuts you off and sends you flying onto the concrete. Immediately, the mind will kick into perception mode: "I'm on the ground!"; "I'm injured!"; "My bike is mangled!"; and most likely, "That guy is a reckless a*&#$@%!"

Now, suspend disbelief for a moment and imagine you can fly. If you knew you could have an eagle view of your environment while soaring with the wind, would you ever actually get on a proverbial bicycle? Would you willingly choose to narrow your field of vision and put yourself in harm's way (perceptive), or would you elect to catch the wind's current, expand your view, and play with the magic at your disposal (*pre*ceptive)?

When working with affinity and the art of being *pre*ceptive, you are unleashing the Law of Potentiality so you can soar. You are deconstructing matter in order to get to the heart of what matters. You are shifting from the mental plane to the Universal plane and in so doing, you are aligning with the alchemy of your soul. In conjunction with the supernatural frequency of the Grid, you are moving away from the falsity of a construct that cannot hold quantum mass and are instead architecting the foundation of your joy.

While unburdening and aligning with the Law of Potentiality, you may feel lost or perhaps listless. But these thoughts are only the mind learning to let go of *how* it once protected you—by rooting you into a manufactured environment. With your ego and mind in the present moment of your Walk, they are learning to respond to your higher frequency, in turn forming a new *pre*ceptive constitution that aligns with your expression.

The purification process releases unnecessary weight and static from your frequency, which can make you feel as though you've been uprooted and are now without grounding. But that couldn't be further from the truth.

As the winds gently swirl around you on the path you're courageously forming, know that you cannot be swept from it.

In many ways, you are more grounded than you've ever been, seeing as through the process of taking your first steps, you've untangled your heart from the grip of fear. Now, there is nothing fear can do to convince you that you might fail because to do so would be an impossibility: the Law of Potentiality states, "The resonance of each unique frequency is perfect in all stages of attunement." This means you can't—in any way—fail; you can't hit a wrong note. Or as my mentor plainly puts it, "You cannot *not* get where you're going."

It's essential to stay present on your Walk while allowing the feelings of being groundless to fill you with thoughts of possibilities rather than alarm. Know you are no longer bound to the false identity that has kept you chained and unable to move, to explore. Understand you are not at the mercy of what your mind chooses to perceive. But rather, you are free. And as weight continues lifting from your shoulders, releasing debris from your very cells, feel your feet lift off the path until the wind takes you in its arms.

Then, if only for a moment, fly.

PIQUE TO PEAK

Becoming alchemical will change you in myriad ways, chief among them being what you consider important—what resonates and vibrates within your very cells. Things once sparking your interest will shift as you move from being *piqued* to reaching your *peak*.

As your mind and ego retune, thereby dropping a manufactured identity, you will notice a soul focus entering into your consciousness, a kind of compass unto which all thoughts and intentions must align. You will move away from the ego's push/pull, or forcible piquing of your interests in areas that keep you from that which you are born to express.

Examining the act of being piqued is vital in that it often drives what we would consider our passion. Distilled, pique is to passion what spark is to flame. And while stoking a fire can be exhilarating, there is a fine line between being warmed and being burnt. Passion consists of ions that pass—they come in like lions then leave a fiery trail of destruction in their wake. This means we must mind the presence of passion in our thoughts and lives lest we be led to passion's counterpart: obsession.

From an origin perspective, the word *passion* embodies suffering and enduring. Therefore, it's not at all the rapturous and emotionally fulfilling experience we assume, and instead, often causes us to fixate—or obsess—on the *absence* of our passion: "Why haven't I attained that person/place/thing?" or "My life would be more fulfilling if I had that person/place/thing." When in a state of preoccupation, we are led to the threshold of obsession and once in its grasp, the path to bitterness and suffering is swift and resolute.

Many, if not most, confuse passion with purpose. In truth, neither is ideal for aligning with that which we are born to express, as passion leads to obsession while purpose invites the ego to build papier-mâché scenery around a supposed identity: "This is my purpose" or "I was born for this." Once in this space, we have entered into rigidity and have locked into the mental plane where our magical and supernatural[chemical] abilities are inaccessible.

Both passion and purpose are impermanent and differ from expression in that they are inflexible linear constructs, whereas expression is cosmically atomic and therefore agile, responsive, and interactive with its environment. Expression consists of ions in a neutral state co-creating at an alchemical Universal level, in turn constantly engaging in a dance with the Law of Potentiality. When locked in the linear track of passion, we are misaligned with the Law of Potentiality and unable to manifest our ever-evolving true expression.

The element of air is unique in its ability to level-set the spirit's and soul's relationship with expression. While forming your path and learning to let the wind provide lift beneath your *Wings*—Willing Integration Nullifying Gravitational Significance—you will leave the oppressive Force of the mind's and ego's gravitational pull and slip into the current of expression.

The element of air separates then recharges your cellular structure, resulting in you being born anew. The separation removes mortar-like debris (obsession, bitterness) and replaces them with air-filled pockets (willingness, openness) that cushion your spirit's cells to form a more responsive and nimble ionic structure. Once expanded and realigned, those ions are recharged and aligned with Source light, which brings all elements into balance while anchoring the ionic field to the Grid.

Once within the slipstream of the Grid's current, passion will alchemically transform into fusion, which is the fuel expression utilizes to co-create and manifest. Fusion comingles with imagination then expands into the vastness of that which you are born to express. Whereas passion is passing and based in suffering, fusion is an outpouring of energy that unites and blends into the boundless potentiality of Universal flow.

Universal flow and Source light are fused with an omni-dimensional Grid, which translates to an environment that embodies all matter, regardless of its evolutionary phase or origin. This differs in how most view and experience the world around them, which is in a limited three-dimensional manner: "I think therefore it is" (mental plane); "I feel therefore I act" (emotional plane); or "I identify therefore I am" (ego plane).

The process of alchemical transmutation frees us from the confines of a three-dimensional existence and expands our Universal connection into an

omni-dimensional experience. During this transformative phase and while continuing to unburden, we enter
into the depth of what the Void encompasses, which is
learning to embrace our polarity.

All matter and its respective building blocks consists
of both light and dark, or rather, shadow. It's important
to understand that these concepts have been commer-
cialized and bastardized to represent the platforms of
good and bad, concepts that are neither accurate nor
constructive on your path to true expression. Polarity
is created by the Universal anchor points of light (that
which is *embodied* Source resonance) and shadow (that
which is *disembodied* Source resonance).

Touching down onto the earthen path that leads to
the top of the mountain, let's explore the example of a
tree along the path, with its long wooden arms reaching
toward the sky. Without an equally sized set of roots,
the tree would list then eventually topple onto its side.
Therefore, if the tree's roots fail to extend into the richness of the soil (shadow) as well as reach toward the sun
(light), it will either limit its growth or not survive at all.

We can figuratively liken soil to shadow in that it's
light disembodied, but that doesn't mean it's *without*
light. Within the dark soil—or earth—are nutrient- and
light-rich particles crucial to our survival; soil is also the
fundamental element of grounding. Within the frame
of our tree metaphor, we can see how the sun—light
embodied—provides a different, but equally important

set of nutrients. Completing the picture, we understand that the tree is best suited with access to both light and shadow (sun and soil) and in the center of its polarity, whereby both its roots and branches are equal in depth and reach.

This center point, or midway peak, is the goal for optimal balance and alignment. Finding our peak between light and dark allows us to call upon the cosmic, atomic, ionic, and photonic nutrients of the Grid, which is the most powerful method for aligning with that which you are born to express. Staying in the resonance of our peak allows us to develop our ability to balance on the edge of change, which, along with accepting *what is*, paves the way to consistently being in flow.

Moving from being piqued and ruthlessly driven by your passions to reaching your peak and resonating with Universal fusion will result in the ability to attain balance while embracing the flow of that which you are born to express. With the heart, soul, mind, and spirit all supported by the element of air, you can explore your center point, your peak, while continuing the unburdening necessary for ascension.

The element of air teaches us that we are in a state of constant change, and in learning to develop dexterity around this Universal truth, we are instantly aligned with the Law of Potentiality. Leaving passion behind and stepping into the flow of fusion as we move toward the balance of our peak brings us into oneness with our alchemical truth: embracing change is the path from *what is* to *what's next*.

So, the Walk has led you here to the top of your mountain, to the peak of your existence where you can see all that is. This is the 360-degree view of the vastness of your existence, the alchemical flow of your spirit, and the unencumbered potentiality of your expression in every direction. And as the sun dips below the horizon and twilight softly drapes the landscape, let the winds of change embrace you. Know you are infinite, beautiful, and courageous. Understand that both your light and your shadow create a kaleidoscopic reflection that radiates outward like a beacon in the darkness.

See the white flame of fusion in your hand and as you raise your palm toward the sky, notice that below, at the base of your mountain, thousands upon thousands of white flames are appearing to illuminate the coming night. These are prismatic particles of the Universal Grid. They are the star-dusted matter that make up all we are and will become. They are here to remind you that you are not, nor have you ever been, alone.

HOW TO MOVE THE MOUNTAIN

Grid Focus: Self-assessment
Elemental Phase: I am but a mountain peak.

- Imagine yourself at the top of a mountain peak; it can be as high as you like with whatever terrain makes you feel the most serene.
- Feel the air around you. Let it rustle your hair, tickle your ears, and brush your skin. Know you are safe where you are; know you are powerful in your ability to reach this mountain peak.
- See the base of the mountain in your mind's eye along with the dark, rich soil that rests there. Honor and appreciate the nutrients the soil offers the vegetation as well as the platform it provides for the mountain's structure.
- Feel the last of the day's sun rays caress your skin until you fully comprehend the purity of the center point: feeling the earth beneath you, strong and nutrient-dense, as well as the sun above you, warm and life-giving. You are clear that living in both light and shadow offers you the opportunity for a peak existence.
- From the depths of the soil, allow your shadows to begin rising. See the shadowy, cloudy air rising from the soil and notice how comfortable you feel while watching it surface. Play with the sensation of seeing beauty in the shadowy smoke, and embrace that this

disembodied light is part of you. Recognize that it makes you, you.

- Find appreciation for your shadows, as they provide depth; your roots can only go as deep as the shadow you acknowledge. Explore the feeling of bliss while you honor the light inside you—light that is both embodied and disembodied.

- Know that all of your experiences have led you to this peak; they merge into either embodied or disembodied light in order to create the polarity in which you will stay balanced.

- Let go of associating people or circumstances with the shadows, seeing as disembodied light is beyond the genesis of its creation. It is now simply particle-ized matter that exists inside you so as to inform your journey and foster your balance within the resulting polarity.

- Notice how weightless you feel, like you are floating. Let every cell in your body marinate in complete and total acceptance. Know you are kaleidoscopic in your light, made of myriad colors, a rainbow of photonic projection.

- Celebrate the colors of your own being and feel thankful that you are blessed with the prismatic reflection of the Universe. Stay with this visualization as long as possible, seeing your array of colors reflecting outward into the coming night like beams of multicolored light.

- Fall into a sense of wonder with all the colors that make you, you.

STAGE THREE

The Rising

ELEMENT: **FIRE**

"The most powerful weapon on earth
is the human soul on fire."
—FERDINAND FOCH

CHAPTER SEVEN

Firestorm

AS YOU CONTINUE YOUR JOURNEY, let's carry over the components of the Grid assessments' visuals. Imagine you're sitting at the top of your mountain peak and as the sun dips below the horizon, you watch night fall and are comforted by the thousands of glowing white flames along the mountain's base. At your back, warmth beckons and when you turn around, you notice a glowing orange light shining from a wide circular opening in the mountain's top, as if the mountain had been cored.

A thick set of vines clinging to the opening's rocky rim form a net-like ladder that leads down into the mountain's cavernous internal structure, at the center of which is a raging fire illuminating the plant-lined walls. Without hesitation, you descend the vine-made ladder, feeling calm and tranquil as you listen to the crackling fire and let its penetrating warmth infiltrate your skin.

Touching down on the graveled surface of the cave floor, you face a column of flames shooting up toward the mountain's opening, knowing this crimson wild fire is part of you. This blazing inferno was lit by the sparks of Source's light in combination with your heart and represents the divine fuel instilled within you by Universal Force.

The closer you move toward the fire, the hotter it becomes, and as you watch it burn, the flames deepen in color. Having moved through the element of air, your cellular and ionic structures have been realigned and expanded. During this process, encrusted and previously trapped debris is released. The mortar-like pieces breaking off and falling away expose buried oppression and rage, which manifest as a blood-infused form of your heart's core element: fire.

When balanced, heart fire is violet-white, and the purer you become, the cleaner it will burn until it appears like violet-tipped vapor. But in order to attain balance, you must first accept and honor the oppression and rage causing your heart's clear flame to run red. To do this means understanding that the fire inside you is complex in both function and volatility. It's of the utmost importance that you choose how your fire is fueled, as that drives Grid alignment and forward motion toward that which you are born to express.

Breaking down the concepts of oppression and rage require detachment from what your mind believes is their origin. The perceived genesis of the rage being released is of no consequence and there is little value in allowing the mind to surface associated events, as these internal opinions and judgments are coming from a limited three-dimensional view that often distorts clarity.

The Universal principle of Oneness is that there is only *one* primary connection you are having at any given moment, and that is the union with self. *Self* is a form of materialized matter than encompasses the spirit inhabiting your humanistic profile, or Source Embodied Light Form. All interactions and experiences are based on this sacred relationship and if it's not treated as such, it invites threads of *Self*-betrayal into what would otherwise be a *Love*-woven union.

Manipulation or betrayal of the union with *Self* causes calcification that presents as disconnection from the soul, heart, and spirit. This triad of blocked energy creates discord in the triangulation and purity of your unique resonant signal and relationship with *Self*. Over time, that dissonance lowers your frequency and pulls you away from that which you are born to express. Lack of alignment with expression leads to static in your connection to the Grid (Universal Flow), and once out of the Universe's slipstream, you become stuck.

The soul, heart, and spirit are designed to resonate in divine expression and when not vibrating with the

Grid's light frequency, they collect debris. This layer of debris traps unreleased expression, which manifests in the Natural (physical plane) as rage, bitterness, and oppression toward *Self* and others.

When we're in a state of rage, the heart sends out pulses of light in an attempt to shake off the forming debris. This action drives the pang of intuition we often feel when misaligned with our expression: "Don't stay in this job"; "Get out of this relationship;" "You're not doing what you were born to do"; and so on.

If left unchecked, the personality will take over and with the ego's help, force an identity to manifest, thereby choking the heart's signal. Although inauthentic and not aligned with true expression, this identity—and corresponding false purpose—cements itself into the mind and convinces the mental structure to preserve its existence at all costs.

As a defense mechanism, the soul, heart, and spirit send thunder-like pulses of light in an attempt to break through the mental structure's blockade; in essence, driving us to be at war with our very *Self*. The turmoil resulting from this battle manifests in myriad ways: emotional abusiveness, unchecked aggression, addiction, bitterness, despair, depression, judgment, exhaustion, and the list goes on. When in this state, we are cut off from our own light and tyrannically ruled by the iron fist of our false identity.

The root of the word rage is *madness* or to be *rabid*,

both indicating a form of *ill*ness and *dis*ease. We often hear others coming in contact with those enmeshed in this internal battle hurtling generalized insults at them, such as "He/She is dreadful" or "He/She is evil." Both of these observations are true, but not in the way they are being implied.

When at war with *Self*, we are not dreadful—we are dread-*filled*. When locked in a standoff with ourselves and cut off from our soul, heart, and spirit, we are not evil; rather, we are living backward: e-v-i-l = l-i-v-e. When we are at the mercy of the mind, we will never actually *experience* mercy because the purpose the mind has imposed upon us is out of flow with that which we are born to express.

Living within the mind's construct, we become enraged. That rabid state will degrade our connection to the light until our soul, heart, and spirit send a pulse so strong that it knocks us to our knees. This photonic, electromagnetic pulse shuts down all systems and forces a kind of *Self* reboot where we are realigned, brought into balance, and placed back in Universal flow. The amount of time we've been living within the mind's false construct dictates the level of intensity experienced during reintegration with our soul, heart, and spirit.

As part of this process, the elements within you begin seeking balance. From an elemental perspective, the work thus far has led you through the stages of: water, bringing clarity and *Self*-reflection and air, providing release from the mind's gravity while electromagnetically refining your ionic structure. Now, fire will begin burning off calcified debris and melting the false foundation of the mental patterns from which you are destined to be freed.

In large part, the freedom you'll attain requires untethering your heart from the toxicity of undigested anger. Moving through the further stages of elemental alignment initiates decoupling from anger, but there is a conscious counterpart required to transition into full detachment.

First, it's essential to identify the functions and interactivity between anger and fury. Anger is used by the ego as a way to distort and suppress the signal of pain or hurt coming from the heart. Essentially, anger is a lid the ego—with help from the mind—places on top of perceived pain as a measure of self-preservation. This action of *canning* heart-based wounds doesn't allow the inflictions to properly release or heal. The greater the wound being canned, the stronger the ego seals the lid, which results in the heart being disconnected from the soul and spirit.

Beneath the lid, pressure builds as the heart seeks to express and reunite with the soul and spirit. Combining with the festering toxicity of the canned wounds, acidity forms and begins eating away at the encasement created by the ego. Technically, this acidity manifests as a byproduct of the psyche understanding the structural integrity is compromised, which is when acidity rises to the surface and becomes fury.

Fury, which is defined as a *state of violent mental agitation*, combines with suppressed anger to form a combustible substance that eventually breaks the seal, forces the lid to release, and allows the build-up of toxicity to dislodge. This flood of suppressed pain and untended wounds is one of the most beautiful things you will experience on the Walk because it is a time of absolute and radical authenticity with *Self*. Now, you have passed into the territory of *Self*-intimacy, and there is nothing more powerful than getting to know the raw majesty and purity of your own heart.

Distilled down, we need to recognize that anger is a secondary response to a primary wound. It is not actually an emotion—it's a state of ego (as opposed to a frame of mind or state of being). Anger, as an impetus for action, is neither constructive nor real. It will only serve to compound the pain or wound it's being used to cover.

In practice, we are never really angry—we are only ever wounded. Through the Grid Work, we will eventually learn that we are not capable of truly being wounded, seeing as *Self*-intimacy posits that we are our own Source of healing.

Simply put, it's not about anyone or anything else inflicting pain upon us, but about how thoroughly we decide to support and care for ourselves within our relationship with *Self*. Taking this a step further, we will come to understand that within Oneness, it is never about another person because we are not separate; there is no *me* as a separate entity from *you*. There is only a unified gathering of light; the *We*, or Wake-initiated Energy, aligned with Source.

The core truth is this: you are a gift. You're a stunning starlit entity born to express a celestial beam of light, and there is a responsibility that comes with wielding that kind of magic. First and foremost, you are your own keeper. The depth of your expression can only echo the thoroughness of your *Self*-care, and as you honor your light, so will others honor theirs. This is the nucleus of Oneness, shattering the illusion of separation and understanding that all individual beams of light are necessary to illuminate the night.

You are a light, but we, as a Collective, are *the* light.

TRIAL BY FIRE

In relentlessly seeking an identity, our egos often convince us that we are our pursuits, passions, or accomplishments. And if any of these false constructs are not suitably stable, the ego will latch on to the one thing it knows we all possess to some degree or another: anger. It doesn't matter how positive our disposition appears, we all have repressed pain or untended wounds, which means anger is ever-present, even if unconsciously.

The ego revels in an identity of anger seeing as it's a naturally inflamed state: "No one messes with me"; "I don't take gruff from anyone"; "I know who I am and what I'm about;" "Nobody pulls a fast one on me;" and so on. These familiar inflations are a welcomed suit of armor for the ego, and it will hold on to them above all else.

We've already established that the ego is primitive and a leftover aspect of our primordial DNA. We've also touched upon the fact that it's imperative not to focus on the ego as an enemy, because when channeled properly, as it was intended, it's a useful ally. As you move through the burn-off phase of releasing repressed anger and fury, the ego will respond by attempting to clamp down the lid your psyche—by way of your spirit—has removed.

It's at this point that you will give your heart and its crimson flame permission to take the lead. You must consciously step aside and allow your heart, spirit, and soul to vibrate in their natural state, which is alignment with Source. During this calibration, you will walk through a wall of fire that the ego will find terrifying.

This terror is not your reality—it's your ego's reality and it requires you to know the difference. The burn-off of anger, fury, and wound-based debris does not need you to drive the process in order for it to occur. In fact, it's just the opposite. The calmer and more removed you remain, while watching the fire inside you digest the festering aspects of your structure, the smoother the evolution will be.

During burn-off, we need to anchor into our hearts and move into a space of radical *Self*-trust. As the relationship between heart, soul, and spirit are forged, the psyche will inform the newly bonded trio (heart, soul, and spirit) of any untended wounds it feels may threaten prospective growth. The psyche's channel of communication is outside the directives of the mind and refines the Grid current inside us while strengthening our relationship with *Self*, thereby allowing our wounds to heal.

The more unified the heart, spirit, soul, and psyche become, the less ego feels it has a platform from which to rule. Ego then wildly searches for an identity to construct, but at this point has neither the materials nor the labor force to build another false profile. It is here that the ego will fall into a state of terror, and eventually a form of primal death.

Although the ego may be embroiled in this death-come-metamorphosis, you need do nothing, seeing as the ego's transition has nothing to do with *you*. What's dying is its false construct, its lie. But underneath that falsehood is the truth of your expression, which will emerge and take on Source resonance. This is where you can begin forging the new structure with the violet fire of your heart.

Once exposed to the burn-off of the wounds it suppressed, the ego will transition from terror to withdrawal. It will retreat and attempt to regroup in the hopes of finding a way back to what it deems is its purpose, which is to keep you safe by constructing false identities and constructs around what it incorrectly perceived as your fragility.

Here we see the inner workings of ego's misguided pursuits, in that it assumes you *are* fragile. After experiencing its metamorphosed form of death, the ego will stay in withdrawal attempting to regenerate the false constructs it believes are necessary to protect you. With the ego in withdrawal, the heart can take its rightful place while calling upon the wisdom of the soul and the light-filled current of the spirit to realign you with Source.

Even though in withdrawal, ego is tapped into the current of your being and as you align, it will sense that it must find a way to exist within the new paradigm. Ego has its own form of intelligence and once it comprehends that it's been exposed via the process of burn-off, the ego will recognize that the fragility it perceived was not within you, but rather, its place *inside* you.

The ego will recognize that you are not at all fragile and are in fact powerful beyond measure. And once it has accepted this, the ego will move from needing to defend its constructed falsities to learning to uphold the absolute truth of your magical[chemical] nature. Once it has emerged from withdrawal, the ego will shed its false shell, in turn creating a petrified, stone-like version of its former identity. It can then use this stone-like shell as a platform to regrow and align with that which you are born to express.

From terror to withdrawal to petrification, the ego has its own path of evolution, one apart from your Source unification journey. Therefore, the key to weathering burn-off is to let the ego transition without your interference. For ego and *Self* to coexist, ego must agree to let go of the attachment to, and the creation of, false structures. In the shedding of its proverbial shell, the ego disengages from the belief that you are too fragile to be safe in the world without its help, in turn paving the way for *Self*-reliance.

When ego emerges from its isolation and sees that you are not only intact, but also thriving, it understands in real time that you do not require its protection to survive. Once this has taken place, the ego will accept Universal alignment as its primary directive and your heart can then guide the ego into accepting that safety comes when it merges into Universal flow.

With anger and fury in burn-off and ego's subsequent transitory passage through terror, withdrawal, and petrification complete, the psyche is given a chance to breathe and realign with Source. Architecturally, ego detaching from the main structure allows the psyche to create a light-bearing bridge between your soul, spirit, heart, and physical body. Once reintroduced, your ego will now be housed at the center of this bridge, in essence, under the vigilant supervision of your spirit.

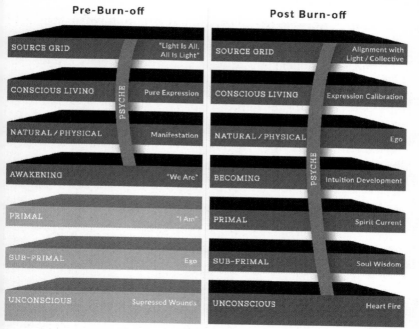

Does this ensure you will never again experience the telltale signs of ego's presence? It doesn't. But it does ensure that you're wise to ego's tendencies and that you've allowed checks and balances to be put into place. Knowing you are safe and embedded within the net of *Self*-trust, you can continue letting your surfacing wounds heal.

As past pain and wounds move through burn-off, you'll no longer experience pain in the same manner, seeing as the ego has changed the way in which it seeks to protect you. Therefore, you are more awake to the pain of others and how it manifests in their relationships to both themselves and you. Your response and reaction mechanism is newly driven by compassion rather than ego, a result of having gone through burn-off and recognizing the suppression of pain in others.

Metaphorically, you can liken it to a topographical sonar detector: the healthier you become, the more clearly you can read the ionic and psychological structures of others—not as a way of judging them, but as a way of offering them compassion and a lifeline of light.

This doesn't require becoming a doormat to those in pain—it requires staying aligned with your true expression and light-filled current. For the mere impact of you standing within your expression and resonating your unique signal will profoundly affect those seeking Oneness. They will feel the ping of awakening just by being around you, because you are expressing as *you*.

HOW TO MOVE THE MOUNTAIN

Grid Focus: Self-assessment
Elemental Phase: I am crimson flame.

- Imagine you are sitting in front of a tall column of crimson flames. Innately, you understand this beautiful fire is part of you and that it is ultimately fueled by your heart.
- Feel the fire's warmth seep into your skin, your sinew, your bones, and your marrow. Allow the sensation to infiltrate you so completely that you feel you actually *are* the fire.
- Play with the idea of being fire: How does it feel to burn, what do you see, what is your source of fuel?
- At the center of your chest, feel a growing circle of warmth and sense your heartbeat getting stronger; a great and rhythmic drum that beats in perfect time. Concentrate on the beat of your heart until everything else in your mind's eye fades.
- Slowly ask your breath to fall in time with the beat of your heart. Ask your lungs to come into alignment with your heart's rhythm.
- Once you feel your breath and heartbeat in rhythmic time, gently ask your blood and cells to absorb the warmth of the fire before you.
- Let the crackle and hum of the fire seep into your blood while the beat of your heart grows ever

stronger. In this moment, feel the raw power of your spirit coursing through your veins. Know you are fueled by sacred fire and ask your body to release all that is keeping your flame from burning violet-white.

- Give your mind space and time to respond, and make no judgments about what appears in your mind's eye. Let your psyche use your thoughts as a canvas. Feel how safe you are in your own care. Know that you, and you alone, are your greatest gift to yourself.

- Stay with the images in your mind's eye as long as they continue to manifest. Once you feel they are ready to be released, carefully ask them to move into the flames.

- Watch the images transform rather than burn, and see each piece of your mind's creation morph into a dancing flame. Notice one thing forging itself into another.

- Know you have the power at any time to free yourself by way of the fire in your heart. Feel the freedom as the debris you've called forth willingly submits to the beauty of your heart's flame.

- Stay with the visualization as long as possible until every last piece has become a dancing flame. Thank yourself and honor your courage. Let the warmth of the fire embrace your soul.

- Then, if you can, lie down and cocoon yourself in the visualization of the fire as you're lulled by its comforting warmth.

CHAPTER EIGHT

Ring of Fire

THE CRIMSON COLUMN OF FIRE present when you first entered into the sacred space of your heart offered an opportunity to burn off trapped rage while healing untended wounds. You have taken the stagnant and fury-tainted blood from your heart and sent it through a filter in order to be cleansed and repurposed as fuel.

Being at the tail end of this process allows you to see the flames anew, as they transition from blood-red to bright, golden-hued orange. This column of flame will continue burning away the debris dulling your light, while bringing you closer to that which you are born to express. And, in order to complete the process and solidify the ego's newfound role, you will need to step toward, then into the column of fire.

Your first step into the flames will find you shifting into a perspective whereupon you understand that what you were seeing as a column of fire is actually a circle of flames. Meaning, you have walked into a column of fire that is comprised of a ring of smaller flames. Breaking it down, you can think of it as observing versus experiencing: in seeing the column of flame, you are observing the aspects of *a* fire. In entering the fire and standing inside the circle of flames, you are experiencing the aspects of *your* fire.

At the center of the ring is a violet-white glowing light, and the closer you come to its warmth, the safer and more grounded you feel. This pure source of light, almost magnetic in its magical presence, is your heart. In all that you will see on your Walk, it is and shall remain the most transformational thing you'll experience. Your heart is infused with prismatic Source light and if you learn to attune, it will lead you out of the darkness and toward that which you are born to express.

The heart manages the fire inside us and directs it to fuel our unique expression. Through the devices of the ego, mind, and will, we are often pushed from our path until the fire within us becomes vulnerable to misuse, or alternatively, is diminished. Yet, no matter the seeming state of our fire, it is incapable of being extinguished completely. We're designed to, and must, possess all four cardinal elements, as they're the mortar to the matter of our spirit and they cannot be eradicated from our systemic architecture.

The keeper of fire—the heart—has a complex relationship with the ego and when the ego is permitted to dictate our heart's flame, it becomes fractured. Exploring the concept more fully, we see ego suppressing untended wounds, causing anger and rage to build exponentially, and in most cases, unchecked. This toxicity spreads and threatens to erode the heart's connection to Source light and as a result, the heart casts around it a circle of flame, forming a barrier to keep the flood of acidic residue from eating away at what is essentially the pinnacle of our light.

While our heart is always accessible to us, when at the center of this fiery circle, its influence, voice, and alchemical magic are compromised. In its natural state, the heart sends out tiny light-bound tentacles that attach to every sliver of matter than makes us what we are. These tentacles pulse with Source truth and trust, while triangulating with our soul and spirit; for all intents and purposes, heart, spirit, and soul are our *trinity*.

Let us not invoke with this statement the spiritualistic dialogue around the concept. For the purposes of this book, *trinity* is solely inside you and for you. The use of this term is deliberate, in that we are unifying these three aspects and must hereinafter consider them as one: a triangulation of three distinct points, at the center of which lies our wholly formed and light-filled being. This trinity is the platform of our expression; it is the stage upon which we give our expression the freedom to play, discover, and most importantly, resonate.

The courageous act of surrendering to burn-off has given your ego a new purpose, and with your untended wounds healing more each day, you'll begin to feel lighter and closer to your *Self*. It's vital that we address the fact that burn-off and wound-tending are not elixirs to cure all ails. Every one of us carries the trials and tribulations of our lives in different ways, and once the lid to our heart has been released, we can often feel the effects quite intensely.

In this, we need to unify the circle of flame with our heart fire in short order. This merging of burning light— or fire—will assist with our transition into a deeper relationship with both *Self* and Source Grid. Ultimately, leading us into greater *Self*-intimacy and eventually that which we are born to express.

As you embark upon this merging process, you can put weight onto and belief into a principle Universal truth: you are made from, comprised of, and resonate with light. This means that no matter what your human senses, intellect, or emotions falsely show you, there is a light-woven safety net around you at all times. Admittedly, it doesn't always feel this is the case, but that's merely the mind needing to warn you of impending danger, so as to keep you ever-vigilant and ready to survive. It's an antiquated thought pattern by which threads of archaic DNA are still present in our lives, but these fear-based impulses are neither the truth nor your truth.

It warrants addressing that this principle is an application to relationship with *Self* and does not excuse, invalidate, or bypass trauma inflicted upon us by others. We are entitled to our pain as a way of accepting *what is*, but we want to move through that ache and release it by way of burn-off once the psyche lets us know we're ready. Our readiness is often indicated by the ping of feeling something's missing, that we aren't on the right path, or that we feel the urge to enter into betterment and liberation. That is the psyche pinging the unconscious, which happens in tandem with the heart sending out pulses of light to loosen the ego's grasp.

Holding onto pain is a trap the ego often uses to trick us into bondage, and that hurt can be in myriad forms: physical, mental, emotional. Oftentimes, the ego will use our primary pain story as a buttress for the structure of a false identity, whether that be victim or survivor. Treading carefully on a topic deserving thorough explanation, we will learn through utilizing the element of fire that these two resulting aspects of trauma, victim or survivor, are actually one in the same. They are born of, and built from, one impact point: the core wound.

Throughout our lives, we gather an array of wounds, but there is a core wound that first rips us away from the light. That separation is very real to the mind and ego, yet it's not, in practice, an actual parting from Source light. The core wound triggers dormant archaic and primal DNA, which, once awakened, aligns with the ego to form a construct that will keep us safe—or so the ego would have us believe.

Burn-off reveals the core wound, which manifests into the psychological architecture as a core trigger. As a sampling, we may see extreme manifestations of a need for approval, need for control, need for importance, or need for territory. Playing it out, let's look at an individual who grew up in a household without enough resources to feel safe; those resources could be monetary, emotional, or physical. Whatever the display of lack in this individual's life, their core wound forms, then converts into a driving need the ego uses to begin building false structures.

In this case, we may see this individual develop a driving ego need to control, which this person believes will keep them safe from again experiencing the pain and disappointment that caused their original core wound to form. Manifesting in the Natural, this person may react irrationally to minor life changes or losses of perceived control over persons or situations. Yet, what this individual is responding to in a scenario encompassing an apparent loss of control is not truly another person or situation, but to the original—and untended—core wound.

Translated into the dynamic of human relationships, many of us are in a constant state of trigger and only having relationships with the core untended wounds of ourselves and others. It's difficult to know another person, even superficially, until they've awoken enough to recognize their core wound and resulting ego-driven need, or trigger. As a connection point to this view, we begin to understand where conflict gestates. Technically, the root of most, if not all, conflict—or lack of resonance with another—comes from us operating from untended wounds that have forced an ego-driven need and subsequent false identity.

Therefore, in many cases, we are not *out of our minds*—we are *out of our hearts*. We have simply forgotten that we are not our pain story or core wound. We are not what has *happened* to us, rather we are what is *happening*; we are the Collective, merging back into our individual light and ultimately aligning with the resonance of Source. *We* are the most important Universal happening, seeing as the vibration of the Collective increasing connects our hearts and moves us toward awakening and that which we are born to express.

Through the Grid, we are networked with one another, a great and light-filled super Collective; the more resonant our unified signal, the more hearts will be reached and merged back into the light. This is how we move beyond the pain story, the core wound, the false identity, and the conflict that keeps us on our knees; we are only as strong as we are united. From a Universal perspective, unification is the tipping point for wholly organic, significant, and sustainable change.

First, we must merge our protective circle of fire with our heart fire—our heart's light. During this process, any festering debris will be burned away and reduced to the ash we'll use to later nourish our growth, seeing as the most robust forests grow from soil layered with ash. Therefore, it's time to free your spirit and let all that is not aligned with the light be offered up to the fire inside your heart.

This offering up of all that keeps you in bondage will change you at a cellular level. Merging the fires around, and in, your heart forges you with your *Self*, and it is here that you will embody your alchemical *magicianship*. For the Force within you is profound, and in some respects unfathomable from the viewpoint of the human mind. We are all capable of immense feats of magic, and you are no exception. There is nothing you cannot do, there is no path you cannot form, and there is no fire into which you cannot walk.

You are beautiful. You are powerful. You are elemental.

LET IT BURN

Standing in front of the violet-white glow of your heart, with the circle of fire around you, know how incredibly brave you are to be in this sacred space. In merging, or rather, forging the protective circle of fire with the flame of your heart, you will reach the apex of alchemical transfiguration.

Before your heart can accept the flames in the circle of fire, it needs to go through a preparation process, seeing as the fire being absorbed is comprised of an entirely different kind of flame. Ironically, the ring of flames was created to protect your heart, but in order to commence the forging of the two fires, you must do the very thing you were striving to avoid: you must break your own heart.

The molten white-hot center of the heart is the only substance capable of subsuming the flames contained within the circle of fire. Imagine how long each of us have had this protective fire burning, how great the cost of fuel, and how wildly it's burned—perhaps even harming both ourselves and others. This fire has an identity of its own and must submit to the heart in a manner that requires abandoning the very purpose of its existence.

In asking this secondary, ring-shaped fire to give in, it must first be shown that the fire into which it will be subsumed is equally as willing to surrender. There is a kind of invisible shell protecting your heart's Source light and fire. In order to bring your *Self* into oneness, this barrier needs to be removed, it needs to be broken. It's at this point that your heart will unleash the fullness of its heat, its power, and its wounds.

It's here that the heart's previous hurts become visible because we understand that all the energy spent erecting and maintaining the circle of fire failed to protect the heart from being wounded. The fallacy that we can stave off heartbreak, in general, is now clear and present. We are aware in this moment that we have spent a great deal of our lives defending a heart that was already broken, regardless of how high our ring of fire was built.

With this, we explore a fundamental aspect of the Grid Work: there is no such thing as hurt—there is only transformation. What actually causes our wounding is the very act of defending against being wounded, in turn believing we *can* be hurt. As a rudimentary example, hold a toy in front of an infant and let them interact with the object. After a moment, imagine we take the toy away and replace it with a completely different, perhaps less interesting, type of toy. In most cases, the infant will begin examining the new toy and will find ways to interact with the object so as to enjoy playing.

What an infant isn't doing is making up a story about why the toy was swapped with another. Nor does the child fixate on the attachment or memories it formed while handling the original toy. Naturally, the infant accepted *what is*, which was that the original toy had been taken. Then, acceptance was reached and eventually what's next, which was to play with the new toy and immerse into subsequent enjoyment.

An older child, in many cases, would have had an emotionally charged reaction to the original toy being taken. Therefore, at this point, the child is suffering, or hurt, because of a refusal to accept *what is*. This is how our Source-filled or primary state, present in infancy, is altered once the ego comes into the equation. The world around us goes from *this is* to *I am,* and herein lies the need to protect ourselves from being hurt.

What is being left out from a Grid perspective is that when in flow with that which we are born to express, we are at our highest level of vibration. We are comfortable with accepting *what is* and we have—for the most part—shifted our relationship with suffering into a union of acceptance and flow. This unified state *opens* our hearts, which allows us to resonate with the open hearts of others. Meaning, those with closed hearts and over-functioning protection mechanisms are out of flow with our vibration and are therefore not on the same frequency; they are not attracted to our signal.

Even if coming into contact with a person of this ilk results in an unpleasant encounter, once your heart is open, you will see they are operating from both fear and core wounds. With this realization, compassion kicks in and subverts the ego's defense engine. Experientially, on this open-hearted frequency, you are less likely to experience pain and suffering than you are when in a mode of vigilant protection. And you will begin to see that you cannot be hurt unless you are in a state of refusing *what is.*

Distilling the concept to its base, we recognize that accepting *what is* releases us from attachment to *what is not,* thereby moving us into flow. Second, we comprehend that being hurt is a concept invented by the ego as a tool to trick us into complying with closing our hearts—creating a ring of fire—and constructing false identities.

It bears repeating that there are circumstances of extreme trauma that require professional support. Experiencing hurt and pain from severe traumatic instances must be carefully addressed and gently guided by an expert in the field of the respective trauma. To an individual in trauma-based pain, the hurt is very real and it must be treated with great respect and patience.

In picking back up with the distillation of the concept, we explore the idea that rather than hurt, what we're experiencing is a call for transformation. In practice, imagine an individual in a relationship where their partner uses words to control or shame; if this individual rejects the gift of transformation, they will refuse *what is* and enter the realm of suffering. They will *Self*-betray and stay in the relationship out of fear: "No one will love me like he/she does"; "But when it's good, it's really good"; "I know he/she loves me deep down"; "All partnerships go through rough patches"; and the list continues.

These statements are the ego holding this individual in bondage, because the ego feels the person is safer in the relationship than they are in the terrifying world alone. Ego believes two are better than one in fighting for survival and that "the devil you know is better than a devil you don't." Taking it a step further, in many ways, longing for a partner is more about the ego's fear for our survival than it is a single individual truly wanting to be in a relationship.

In our example scenario, the individual staying in the relationship and not accepting *what is* has blocked themselves from the magical[chemical] potential of transformation. Metaphorically, imagine a snake refusing to shed its skin. After a period of time, it wouldn't be able to grow, eventually being suffocated by its own debris. In essence, this is precisely what we do to ourselves when refuting *what is* and, ultimately, declining the Universal invitation to transform.

When snakes are ready to shed, they weave in and out of sharp rocks to abrade, slough, and pull the dead skin away. The rocks are far less comfortable than smooth, warm grass, but intrinsically the snake knows the rocks will eventually lead it to freedom and growth. At times, we too are required to shed our skins via a rock-filled path. But that path also leads to transformation and the more willingly we make the journey, the more streamlined our evolution will become.

In breaking your own heart, you've allowed the deepest wounds and perceived hurts to burn off and turn into pure ash. The membrane encasing your heart is gone and of its own accord, the ring of fire has begun moving inward, tightening around you as it travels toward your heart's violet-white flame. If you stand still, reveling in the beauty of your heart's true light, the circle of fire will pass through you, cleansing your cells as it reaches, then merges into your heart.

Like with the rocks, the ring of flames has shed your skin. With it having burned away, you have renewed your proverbial Source-created flesh and can bask in the mighty fire of your open heart. You are in flow with *what is* and committed to continuing to release the ashen debris floating up and away from your heart's fire.

Once you merge the flames and cease misusing your heart's fire, it will reset to its original state, which is one of stillness rather than action. In its purest form and purpose, fire is the language of the heart. It is the fuel of creativity and the conduit of the spirit's whispers. The fire inside you is meant to warm your heart and stoke your zest for life; it is from your heart's fire that all expression is born.

This unified flame is part of you now, and it will forever fuel the voice of your soul.

HOW TO MOVE THE MOUNTAIN

Grid Focus: Self-assessment
Elemental Phase: I am two flames becoming one fire.

- In your mind's eye, see yourself sitting in front of your heart. Feel the warmth on your face and see the purity emanating from your heart's violet-white fire.
- Know, deep in your gut, that this flame is part of you. You are one. Understand the fire speaks and connects with your intuition like roots to a great tree.
- Believe in the union between you; see yourself reaching out toward your heart. Let it be whatever shape or size it wants. Let your creativity play within the visualization.
- Listen to the subtle crackle of the flames as you continue watching the prismatic light of your open heart fill the space around you.
- See how it feels to have a truly open heart. What weight has been lifted as a result?
- Stay with the release of knowing you are changed, that you are letting go of the wounds that have long held you in bondage.
- Love yourself for having the courage to release and focus on your freedom rather than the details of your wounds. *Know* you are free.

- Expand into the vastness you feel with such an open heart. What do you see? Are colors brighter? Is your mind clearer?

- Sit with the sensation of your newly opened heart as long as possible. Feel the lightness in your chest and imagine light shining outward from your heart and filling the room.

- Gently, ask yourself to open your heart even more. See if you can release any further debris.

- Once you have opened your heart as much as possible, ask the fire in your heart to trust you. Forge a connection with your heart and ask for guidance on how to better listen to its wisdom.

- Then, listen. Let your heart speak and tell you everything it feels. Allow its voice to fill your cells. Listen, until it returns to stillness.

CHAPTER NINE

Ever Poised

THE FIRE OF YOUR HEART will now change to violet. This solitary flame burns clean and true and is fueled by Source light through a steady connection to the Grid. The violet flame of your heart can now work in conjunction with your retuned ego and mind in a manner allowing poise to enter into your ionic field.

Whereas some believe an ego-driven nature projects confidence, those moving into the glow of the violet flame begin to understand that genuine poise is the origin of authentic *Self*-assuredness. *Poise,* defined at a root level, embodies *equal weight, balance,* and *consideration.* Therefore, poise surpasses the ego's version of confidence in that it's anchored in the unity of the Collective; moving us from the ego's and mind's *I am* to the light-based Collective's *Oneness* is.

It's when we cease creating separation and needing to put our own accomplishments before those of others, or misusing our light to outshine those around us that we find lasting peace and belief in our respective *Self*. Poise comes when we recognize that our light, when joined with that of others, connects to light's Source. Meaning, in Oneness with the light from which we are made, we are tapped into the Force of the entire Universe. Once we have experienced this kind of connection and resulting poise, we can begin to comprehend that outshining others is counter to the laws of unity: in diminishing the light of another, we are damaging our own.

Seeing as we're tethered together electromagnetically, if one individual attempts to diminish the light of another, they have succeeded in lowering their own frequency. Thereby, that individual will be vibrating at a level lesser than that of Source and potentially attracting undesired energetic currents. The frequency of the person they intended to outshine remains unchanged, while the individual seeking to diminish them has compromised their systemic integrity by allowing their vibrational level to be reduced.

More crudely stated, it would be as counterproductive as an individual attempting to poison another by drinking the poison themselves. What we see in this metaphor is how ineffective mind's and ego's methods are for creating separation because it has but one result, which is the lessening of the vibration and Collective resonance.

On the other end of the scale, when we seek to raise the vibration of another or to amplify their light, we send an electromagnetic charge throughout the Grid. This light-charged pulse heightens the frequency of the Grid as a whole, seeing as the Collective then boosts the signal and magnifies it through the channel to Source. Distilled down to a base scenario, imagine rather than hoarding or fighting for a piece of pizza in the proverbial pie, instead an individual raises their vibration up and away from the idea of separation and gives their piece to another person.

The conscious choice to unify with the Collective amplifies that individual's signal, in turn increasing the size of the pie tenfold. What we're seeing here is the mind's primal impetus to separate, transitioning into the realm of conscious Oneness, in turn changing "One *for* them means less for me," or the myth of lack, into "One *from* them means all for One," or the Law of Amplitude. Experientially, we are energetically tethered, which means the more individuals awakening to the frequency of Oneness, the higher we vibrate as a whole: "So, as the one (individual), as is the whole (Collective)."

In retuning the mind and ego, and in aligning the elements explored thus far (water, air, fire), you have enhanced your connection to Source Grid and have begun the process of attuning to the Collective. Now, you have access to Universal Force in a profound manner, and that connection will serve to further refine your vibration and relationship with both *Self* and the Law of Amplitude.

This is where you'll gain the very essences of poise: equal weight, balance, and consideration. Equal weight sees you even-footed and grounded, balance gives your heart the space to continue radiating its violet flame, and consideration gives your soul and spirit the freedom to explore the alchemy associated with Oneness.

Our experiences while in the humanistic profile are driven by the level of purity in our connection to the Grid. And our highest vibration while in the humanistic profile can only come from aligning our light with Source, while allowing poise and harmony to infiltrate our cellular architecture. One of the most central principles to understand is that we are not humans experiencing light, rather, we are light experiencing being human, which means the light must come first, as it is the Source matter from which we are made.

If we put the human first and neglect our light, we are out of flow with the Collective and at the mercy of ego delusions and chaos within the primal mind. Taking care of our bodies and honoring the exquisiteness and strength of their design is paramount, but the health of the body is predicated upon the purity of its connection to Source.

Purification has seen the violet flame of your heart healing untended wounds, the spirit enriching its connection to the Grid, while your soul actively aligns with the Collective. But as all aspects of your trinity are attuning, the mind and ego are also attempting to find their place of balance.

Therefore, as we unify and gain perspective away from the ego and mind, it can be tempting to fall into *second force*, which is a channel created by the will: where ego constructs false identities, the will constructs false channels. Second force channels speak more quietly than the ego's false identities, but they still have the potential to create static within the connection to Source. Their primary manifestation peaks around specific concepts such as: "I've completely changed"; "I'm a different person now"; "I'm much calmer than I used to be"; and grandiose statements of this nature.

It's important to detect the notes of separation here, seeing as these statements are all cemented around "I." When going through major transformations, the ego and mind try to find footholds in other, but still familiar, forms. Although you've retuned your ego and mind, they will both go through a pendulum swing from one extreme to the other.

We can attribute the pendulum swing as going from black to white in a spectrum. The ego and mind have swung from one extreme to another and will continue to oscillate until they settle in the midrange, or the gray.

This middle ground is where they'll fully align with the trinity of the heart, soul, and spirit, while tapping into the Oneness of the Collective.

Signals of the pendulum swing are often evidenced by misplaced humility and conciliatory behavior, due to the ego and mind still finding their place in the connection to Source. Meaning, the mind specifically will conjure stories or qualities it *imagines* embody a balanced or composed humanistic profile, because in recently moving away from its primal urges, it doesn't yet know *how* to authentically personify those traits.

Attunement and alignment do not mean being in a constant state of conciliation and agreeability. What they entail is far simpler: our only intention need be Oneness and being in flow with that which we are born to express. The slipstream created by our expression elevates our frequency and brings us closer to the sacredness of our light, and in that, the ego and mind will automatically attune to the vibration of authenticity.

Particularly, when clearing the debris of anger, rage, and the encompassing fury, we can tend to swing into over-functioning kindness and humility—neither of which are balanced states. Rather, they are the mind and ego retuning within their newly aligned structure and seeking opposition from their previous stance. When they do find their midrange—or gray—the mind and ego will be consistently guided by the heart, soul, and spirit, and this will become the filtration system through which all mind and ego impulses will travel.

In the interim, we need to bring into our awareness the fact that this pendulum will continue to vacillate until we have aligned all four elements and attuned fully to the Collective. Humility is, for many in this transformational stage, a trap, as it sees us lowering our vibration and sense of poise. Therefore, rather than humility, what we're seeking is *harmony*.

Harmony gives us humility's gentleness but doesn't sacrifice the power of our connection to the Source Grid. In this, our frequency stays elevated and continues resonating with the Law of Amplitude, while exuding poise and continuing to attune to Oneness. Harmony takes our resonant signal and expands it so as to *neutralize* any dissonance in our electromagnetic field; whereas, humility contracts our signal until it *becomes* dissonant.

Poise and harmony will bridge your transformation and provide a platform on which to stand above your ebbing and flowing seas. Yet, being in a stage of transformation doesn't equate to instability; instead, it means you are courageous enough to harness your elemental abilities and step into the resonance of your expression.

This is a time of great wonder and exploration, and the more you see it as such, the deeper you'll root into the Oneness of the Collective. Within you is the very fire of creation and you were born to light up the night.

GRACELAND

We often hear others say that they have achieved a feat by the "sheer force of their will." While this sounds impressive and perhaps even enviable, it is the result of a false channel through which the will forces our energy toward an imagined destination.

Where the ego creates false constructs as a way of keeping you separate and safe, the will creates a false channel through which your energy is propelled toward a distant destination. Ego resides in the structure of the mind, while the will resides in the structure of the spirit; yet both have primal roots.

Innately, our spirits are born of Source light and fueled by a combination of Universal flow and the spark of creation (Source-ignited alchemy), and in this cosmic form, our spirits are pure. Inside the cord that runs between the spirit and the humanistic profile, there is a conversion point where our light meets the density of our humanness.

Within this conversion point lies the will—the gatekeeper between Source light and heart fire. Where our hearts fuel the engine of that which we are born to express, the will fans the fire of what it presumes can *lead* us to that which we are born to express; in essence, the will is the ever-present chauffeur revving the engine, ready to burn rubber toward a presumed destination, with or without a map.

The will moves us through the sludge-laden terrain

we traverse when not in flow with our expression: "If I can just make it until my year-end bonus, then I'll start my business"; "I can push through until my kids graduate, and then I'll take those classes"; "I'm going to make this relationship work until after the New Year, and then I'll leave."

The objective is to see us through to the destination no matter how battered we are when we get there. In times of the early humanistic profile, we needed a mechanism such as this in order to get from one day to the next. Between harsh weather, food scarcity, and abundant predators, the will gave us the push necessary to go on and to procreate.

As the humanistic profile evolves, the will hinders the engine of progress and immersion into that which we are born to express, because it allows us to subjugate our expression by making it a distant destination. The will's directive of "just push through until you reach the destination" has no association with what we're really pushing through and why, let alone the reason for—or the validity of—the destination we're trying to reach.

For many, the examination of the will's commands is nonexistent, as they believe they're experiencing the true voice of their spirit, which is not the case. The spirit is always seeking to align with Source, in turn bringing you into attunement with that which you are born to express. Therefore, the spirit will not aimlessly push you toward a presumed destination, as it's there to ensure you are consistently attuned to the Grid and aligned with your expression. This alignment requires the spirit to watch over your every move, while coordinating with your heart and soul to guide you and elevate the level of your frequency.

Without the will's interference, the spirit speaks through a permeating knowing that rises up and through the walls of your soul: "You were meant for more than this"; "You're not using your gifts"; "He / She doesn't love you the way you deserve"; "If you take that job, it will suck you dry"; and the list continues.

Notice in these examples there aren't any statements pushing a person toward a destination; there are only statements guiding a person into alignment with their expression. In other words, revealing obstacles between the individual and their truest expression. Unhindered, the spirit reveals that the misaligned job will keep the individual from starting their carpentry or craft business, or that the abusive relationship will keep the person's vibration at a lesser level while stunting their creativity, resulting in their gifts being unused.

What the will fails to understand is that expression is not a destination—it's a Universal truth. Expression is always within the present moment and infinite in its possibilities, and it's the most loyal companion you'll ever have. Therefore, you don't reach expression—expression reaches into and through you, because your expression *is* you.

Put plainly, your will is consistently pushing you toward a destination that doesn't exist, seeing as you cannot move away from yourself or the rightness of the present moment. Since you *are* your expression and that expression is part of your light and ionic structure, there is no need to actually *get* anywhere. As with Dorothy in *The Wizard of Oz*, everything you need is in your own backyard—or in the present moment. And the red shoes on your feet are there to remind you that home is three clicks away: *home* being that which you are born to express.

The will's power lies in the tools it uses to build its construct. While Primary Force is the energy and sensory fabric of the Universe, second force is the will's use of that fabric as a way of fashioning a false channel by which to focus our energy toward a destination. This false channel resides outside the cord running between our spirit and humanistic profile. The channel awakens the mechanism of pride within the humanistic profile, and they affix to one another until we become enslaved by our ability to endure or persevere: "He/She can get through anything" or "He/She can hold out no matter what" and so on.

Here is where willfulness becomes a fully formed channel, whereby the destination is more important than the impetus for attempting to reach it. While in this second force channel built by the will and cemented by pride, we are locked out of Universal flow and cut off from *Self*-trust.

It bears repeating: whereas the ego builds false identities to foster separation with the intention of keeping you safe, the will fashions a false channel to keep you striving toward a distant and coveted destination. Yet both serve to either disconnect or take you away from that which you are born to express, because the will and ego fear displacement and ultimately eradication.

Having merged your circle of fire with the flame of your heart, you have weakened the stronghold of the will, and as with the ego and mind, it's seeking a new platform from which to function. Just as egotism has been replaced with poise, your will has no choice but to transform into the liquid light holding the fabric of the Universe in place: *grace*.

Grace is the base cardinal element. It is the purest form of *Love* that exists. And while grace is an exceedingly powerful element, it possesses zero volatility. Grace is the nucleus of Source and resonates at the highest frequency possible. Universal law dictates that, "Because we are of grace, we are in grace," which means that we can call upon grace at any time, in any situation, for any reason.

The violet flame is a derivative of, and direct connection to, grace. And in keeping with our story, it's where Dorothy can click her heels and arrive in the knowledge and safety of her proverbial backyard. However, the aspect of this story that's hardest to accept for Dorothy is *believing* in the power of the shoes and trusting that the power was within her all along.

In our own parallel experiences, we tend to reject the Oz theory because it requires a high level of *Self*-accountability. In order to activate the shoes, we must not only believe they will take us home, but also we must admit we suffered through a difficult journey wearing shoes that *could* have taken us home. And therein lies the key to freeing ourselves from the channel of the will: accepting that we are responsible for our own journey (yellow brick road), ending the belief that things will be better (red shoes) if we only reach a distant destination (the Wizard), because the truth of our expression was always inside us (backyard).

Grace, through the violet flame, is how you light the path to your expression. Having broken and then opened your heart, you have renewed your connection to grace and as part of your transformation, that grace naturally retunes your will and breaks down the second force channel driving you toward countless destinations that don't exist.

As an illustration, if ever you've found yourself in an intense situation or hardship and a wash of calm rushed into your blood and cooled your anger or allayed your fear, that's grace. In the darkest of hours and nights, when something magnificent rises up from the depths of your being, whether it be an idea, solution, sense of encouragement, or simply a ray of light, that, too, is grace.

Some may also consider it resilience, others inspiration; either way, grace can manifest in myriad forms.

Learning to fuel the violet flame of your heart with grace can fundamentally change the course of your life. And infusing your heart with grace means that it will no longer be just *your* life, rather it will be the *life* in your expression. Additionally, grace is the origin of the cardinal elements; therefore, when calling upon grace for the purpose of alignment, all elements within you must, by Universal law, synchronize with the genesis of their creation, which is grace.

At this point, you have passed through the ring of your own fire, courageously aligning your violet flame while renewing your connection to grace. Your frequency is continuing to heighten while your alignment with the Grid strengthens. The fire in your heart burns steady and true as you begin freeing yourself from your will.

The column of fire once before you has become a flame within you, and as you feel the rhythm of your heart beat in time with the Universal pulse of grace, you understand the vastness of your radiance. In knowing you are now the keeper of your own flame, you climb the vine-woven ladder behind you, and then step onto the earthen path that will lead you back down the mountain.

HOW TO MOVE THE MOUNTAIN

Grid Focus: Self-assessment
Elemental Phase: I am the keeper of violet flame.

- As you make your way down the mountain, you watch night continuing to gently fall. Take in the serene beauty and stillness of your surroundings. Know this is a sacred place, one where you met yourself.

- Feel the warmth in your chest as your heart continues to open and make room for the glow of the violet flame. For as long as your mind's eye will hold the image, see the violet flame inside your heart. Imagine you are being purified with every beat of your heart.

- Know the essence of grace is infiltrating your spirit, your very cells. See liquid light moving through your marrow, bones, veins, and blood, until you feel you are comprised of grace.

- With each step down the mountain, watch the dusk turn to night and take solace in the warmth of the flame inside you and feel the soft earthen path beneath your feet.

- Notice how safe you feel, how weightless. Spend time seeing yourself walking on the path, and find joy in your bravery.

- Observe, that like a trick of the eye, it almost seems your skin glows. As though the flame inside you is so bright that your flesh can scarcely contain it.

- Let your thoughts drift to all that you have elected to let go. Feel the wounds inside you healing and covering over with grace-infused skin.
- Understand that your need for anger is gone, and let your poise rise up and anchor you in the sacredness of your own light.
- Spend time with the feeling of harmony coursing through your soul. Recognize that you are one with Source light, unified in Oneness.
- Take as long as you need to descend the mountain. Let your imagination run wild with scenery, sounds, animals, or whatever it is you choose to see on your path.
- Once at the base of the mountain, see a tree line before you as a waft of sweetly scented earth tickles your nose.
- Breathe the fresh air, feel the violet flame warming your heart, and follow the path into the majestic forest.

STAGE FOUR

The Becoming

ELEMENT: **EARTH**

"When we think of the sky, we tend to look up,
but the sky actually begins at the earth."
—DIANE ACKERMAN

CHAPTER TEN

Into the Woods

THE ELEMENT OF EARTH aligns with cognizance, which is the elevated configuration of our mind after we've begun to awaken. This is where our primitive mind attunes to the vibration of Source and opens to receive knowledge from the Grid, awareness from Source light, and the ability to recognize togetherness, or the Oneness of the Collective. Cognizance is, at its base, a super-charged alchemical epicenter that will combine all the elements necessary to resonate within the frequency of that which we are born to express.

But it's important to note that the primal mind, even with cognizance in play, will continue to exist in some form, as it's an embedded feature of our humanistic profile. As we further awaken, cognizance will resonate with Source frequency and allow us to work within a space of greater awareness, in turn giving us visibility into the pitfalls of the primal mind.

As we enter into the final cardinal element of earth, let's allow ourselves creative latitude as we take a journey into our imagination. Inviting creativity into our alignment process is essential, as it marries both sides of the physical brain while anchoring the alchemy of cognizance into the conscious mind. If you can, immerse as fully into the visualization as possible; the more thoroughly you participate, the higher your frequency will vibrate. Now, let's go!

Night has fallen and as you stand at the base of the mountain, you take a deep breath and delight in the sweetness of the air. The moon is bright, almost as though a companion sun, and you feel grounded by the earthen path beneath your feet.

There is a graceful calm that permeates your entire body and you can feel the heightened level of your frequency vibrating within your soul. Your skin is radiating a soft glowing light and you illuminate the space around you as if celestial matter inhabiting flesh.

Before you, there is a line of immense trees, two of which have their canopies intertwined like they are forming a forested door. Continuing along the path, you make your way toward the tree line using the moon as your guide.

Once at the forest's entrance, you notice the path leading into the forest is lined on either side with small, floating glass spheres containing neon-blue light. Upon closer inspection, it appears the spheres contain live electric currents that send spindly tentacles toward the sides of the glass like octopuses made of light.

Passing through the trees, you follow the path into a lush forest and notice that the path is more circular than straight, like it's part of a greater earth-carved circle. The forest around you is magical and radiates a storybook quality as though having sprung from the pages of a fairytale. Everything feels wildly alive: trees, flowers, branches, and underbrush all leaning in just enough for you to know they're longing to be at your side.

The forest is filled with the sounds of birds, crickets, trickling water, and the rustling of the trees; night is awake and whispering to you from every direction. Walking deeper into the forest, you begin feeling the electricity from the spheres charging your blood until it seems neon light runs through your veins.

There is a mild buzzing in your bones letting you know that your frequency is elevating, and the farther you walk into the forest, the more penetrating the vibration becomes. The soft neon light from the spheres illuminates your earthen path. As you breathe in the sweet night air, you can't help but feel you and the forest are one.

To your right is an ancient-looking oak tree with thick branches that sprawl outward, and several of the trees' giant roots are visible as if the forest's soil can barely hold them. You stop walking and marvel at the tree, feeling its presence as if it were an old friend with whom you share a trove of memories.

A few of the trees' lower branches gently sway, dipping down and brushing against your skin, and as they do, you feel your heart, soul, and spirit align. While communing with the oak, you come to understand that this forest is your awakening, your cognizance: you are on the path that will lead you to *you*.

The oak represents your spirit, which is comprised of a vast network of deep roots and reaching branches that connect to the Grid. The glowing light being cast from your skin is your heart fire fueled by grace. The spheres lining the path contain Source light that has been combined with the current of the Grid and the vibrational consciousness of the Collective to form what is essentially a small Source-powered battery your soul can use to recharge your Walk when you're fatigued or have been out of flow for a lengthy amount of time.

Taking the concept further, within the denser aspects of the humanistic profile—such as primitive impulses, ego-constructed false identities, and enslavement by the will—we are forced to encapsulate Source light. Primarily, this is due to our bodies requiring us to aggregate the light in small doses until such a time as we're ready to transform into an elemental and alchemical state.

Our ionic and electromagnetic structures hold these batteries in permeable cellular spheres, allowing the density of our humanness to access the light without wholly absorbing it, which in an out-of-flow state would short-circuit the mind's connection to the network of the heart, soul, and spirit.

Within your forest visualization, the path upon which you're walking represents time. Earth, as a planet and purely because we're physically on it, *appears* to have adhered to the concept of time. However, earth, as an element, opposes the mental construct—and concept—of time. In fact, time, as a linear theory, does not exist. The linear theory of time is something our minds use to keep us in line with the life it *thinks* it's running on our behalf; the mind uses time as either a carrot we must persistently chase toward a goal, or a mode of motivation and justification.

Where the will has you rocketing toward a destination, the mind wishes you to be bound by the concept of time: "There's not enough time in the day"; "I'd meet you if I had time"; "I'm sorry I haven't called you back—I just haven't had time"; "I'd better push so-and-so to get that done before I run out of time"; "I have to pay my bills on time"; and the list can go on indefinitely.

What we're *not* talking about here is becoming irresponsible. Of course, we have to pay our bills on time, complete projects on time, or meet our friends on time. What we *are* talking about is the fact that time as a linear track pulling us along and telling us how to live our lives is *not* its intended function.

Rather than linear, time is circular. And instead of being rigid, time is liquid. Time is the barometer of cognizance and subject to the current of Universal flow in that it too is connected to both Source and the Grid. Whereas our mind uses time as a way of running our lives, our cognizance uses time as a way of *reviving* our lives.

In practice, we may see someone leaving an abusive relationship, quitting a dead-end job, seeking help for an addiction, or getting healthy and after such a lengthy struggle with being stuck, we wonder what finally moved the needle. When we ask, oftentimes we hear: "It was time." And it was. But not because the mind made it so, but because cognizance *revealed* it so.

Akin to the path in our visualization, time circles the inside of our cognizance and creates a kind of force field designed to keep us aligned with that which we are born to express. So the linear theory of time used by the mind is a misrepresentation of the true function of *Time*, or Telekinetic Initiation Manifesting Expression, which is the ping of cognizance letting us know that alignment with our expression is imminent.

The root of the word *telekinetic* is *motion* or *to move*, which doesn't mean forced action or effort. In this context, the definition means to *be* moved at a cognizant, or awakened and aware level, to feel what we're born to express at our fullest capacity; and motion is simply ions moving—our ionic structure working in tandem with our cognizance to fuse with our expression. Therefore,

Time is showing us that we are *moved* by the flow of joy associated with that which we are born to express. Once that inner knowing has been initiated, manifestation of our truest expression becomes imminent.

When out of flow and ruled by the ego, mind, and will, our expression lays dormant within our Universal field. Even though our expression is steadily seeking to align with us, it will not force us into that union, seeing as the light accompanying the fusion with expression would damage the structure of the humanistic profile. This is why the encapsulated *batteries* mentioned earlier exist; we need sustenance and light transfusions until we're ready to step into our full resonance. But before we're prepared for our highest resonance and fusion with true expression, our humanistic profile must first be primed, attuned, and unified in order to vibrate at the level of that which we are born to express, which is where elemental alignment comes into play.

Our expression is sentient and in lying dormant, it's awaiting the moment in which our heart and spirit sense the spark of awakening. Once this spark registers on the Grid, a signal is sent to our soul whereupon the first pings of our expression are received. These gentle waves reverberate within the soul until we become consciously aware of being misaligned with our expression; we may not understand why we're not aligned, or with what we need to align, but we will know it's *Time* to look deeper and consider the possibilities of change.

When we transition into openness and begin seeking our expression just as it's seeking us, we activate cognizance while merging the stored batteries (spheres) within our ionic structure into our humanistic profile, so as to attune to the frequency of Source. This assimilation fosters awakening and eventually a solid connection to Source Grid. And it is here that our expression can initiate our vibrational attunement to the resonance of joy.

In grounding into the element of earth, our mind comes to understand that rather than running our lives with time, it can foster conscious engagement. Meaning, we ask the mind to work with the heart, soul, and spirit to keep us in flow while we do the grounding work necessary to elementally align. As an illustration, rather than, "I don't have time to see a doctor," a scenario in which time is the impetus, we chose *Time*'s counterpart, *engagement*, or sending energy toward that which we are born to express. This changes the mind's dialogue to, "In order to stay within a signal of joy, I choose to engage with my health," realizing that not doing so results in a vessel (body) ill-equipped to align with true expression.

For most cases, *engage* can replace *Time*; and it works in both directions. In situations where the mind tells us, "I don't have time to see that person," the actual dialogue—and cognizant truth—is, "I choose not to engage with that person because when I'm near them, I'm not in resonance with joy." Or conversely, with, "I have to submit that project on time," the actual dialogue is, "I choose to engage with this project because it fosters my financial well-being," which ultimately aligns with the resonance of joy. Swapping *Time* with *engage* shows us our truth in any given moment, circumstance, or scenario.

With this change in mental dialogue, it's more difficult for the mind to pull you along a track whereby it runs your life. In recognizing that *Time* is a function of our cognizance and not a mental construct dictated by clocks and corresponding schedules or time, we encourage our mind to transform into a greater engine of consciousness.

When we alter our dialogue around time, we discover a host of buried truths around what does and doesn't support our resonance with joy. Mostly, this is due to the fact that the mind uses time as either motivator or excuse, and neither puts the alignment where it needs to be, which is in your vibration with joy. From this point forward, notice how your mind uses the traditional concept of time and when it does, you can dig deeper by using *Time*'s engagement dialogue. With this, you'll have a firmer understanding of what takes you away from, or brings you closer to, your resonance with joy.

TRINITY RADIO
Radio waves travel through the air, yet the towers that receive them are grounded in earth. Earth *is* our

grounding, and it's where we plant the seeds that will eventually grow into that which we are born to express.

At this point in the elemental journey, all the aspects of your alignment will *go to ground*. Earth allows the other elements to comingle and unify as you foster further fusion with your truest expression. Within the forest of your cognizance and on your earthen path, you will begin dropping seeds of opportunity and amplification as you continue your Walk.

While the ego, mind, and will find their footing within your higher frequency, your humanistic profile needs to begin attuning to life in the Natural, or physical plane. When we're on our ascension Walk, our heart, soul, and spirit adjust to higher vibration levels rapidly, but for our bodies and minds, it can take longer. One of the most common areas stalling the elevation of our humanistic profiles is static in the frequency of our interaction with others.

Ego and mind, as a primal impulse, seek to separate us from what they view as a *herd*, comprised of those that are "lesser than." Interestingly enough, even nature knows being part of a unified group increases safety and resonance—this is illustrated through the formation of forests, herds, packs, and flocks.

As the heart, soul, and spirit work to align the mind, ego, and will, we'll most likely still operate within our respective triggers. And when in trigger, ego and mind will immediately seek to separate: "He/she is obnoxious"; "He/she is stupid"; "He/she doesn't get it"; and so on.

These are examples of the ego passing judgment so as to separate. Next, the mind will come in and begin grinding down our vibration with a barrage of questions: "Why does he/she act like that?"; "Why does he/she not like me?"; "Why is he/she being rude?"; "Why is he/she doing it that way?"

The mind wants answers to questions that are none of its business and irrelevant to the alignment process. The line of inquiries the mind sends in rapid succession is an archaic function of the humanistic profile once needing to attune to its environment. Today, we understand how as humans we fit into our environment at a base level: we must eat, drink, sleep, breathe, and have shelter and warmth to survive. The primitive impetus to constantly question how to survive is no longer necessary, so the mind's probing questions about our environment, the people in our environment, or *why* they are doing what they're doing are of little significance.

First, it's unlikely we'll ever know why a person makes the choices they do, whether in their own lives or toward us, because they themselves don't understand their choices. Second, their behavior has nothing to do with us: it is never about the other person—it is only ever about our relationship with our *Self* being echoed through others.

People are either in resonance with your frequency or not in resonance with your frequency. And the story stops there. Nothing is gained by judging the person, making them wrong or bad, questioning why they are whom they are, or have done what they have done. You will most likely never find an answer through the machinations of your own mind, nor will you glean clarity from pummeling them with mind-driven queries.

The most valuable communication you will have with others is through the vibration of your frequency. If you are out of resonance with a person for whom you care deeply and cannot *tune in* to them in the present moment, go inward rather than making it about them: "Where am *I* experiencing static in my frequency?"; "Is resonance possible in *my* current state of being?"; "Am *I* in trigger and confusing this person with aspects of *my* trigger?"

These trinity-based inquiries keep the focus on the level of your frequency rather than on the other person being wrong and behaving poorly. When you turn inward and rely on the trinity to align your frequency, the other person will have no choice but to attune to the higher vibration, or energetically, *tap out*. When your frequency is at the level of Source, you are embodying radical authenticity and in that state, there is no possible argument: your alignment is simply *what is*.

If you allow static to lower your frequency while following the carrot of the mind and ego into the rabbit hole of an argument, you have lost the element of authenticity Source offers; you have become out of tune, which will only serve to increase the level of static in any given exchange. When finding yourself in this state, especially while in the newness of your cognizance and current alignment, it's best for *you* to energetically tap out.

In doing so, you are bringing the static into the light and owning your lack of attunement: "I'm not aligned with my authenticity right now and in order to honor the relationship, I'd like to regroup and come back together on this topic" or "Our relationship is important enough for me to internally address what I'm feeling before expressing it." After communicating your statement of attunement, keep your energy as neutral as possible and refrain from making any other comments.

Realize this is a completely alternate way of communicating that takes diligent practice. But it will exponentially increase the amount of time you spend in resonance with joy, seeing as static in relationships are how our frequency is most often compromised. After making an attunement statement and neutralizing static within our own vibration, we will have shifted the frequency of the conversation and corresponding exchange. The other party will have no choice but to align, or tap out because their respective trinity will recognize that yours has tuned into Source, and when light is the pinnacle of an exchange, static cannot be present.

Of course, there are complex variables existing in relationships, such as the type of relationship, circumstances surrounding the relationship, signal clarity of the other person in the relationship, and the respective level of awakening of the other person in the relationship. But all interactions can be distilled down to a single base: in the present moment, there is only resonance or non-resonance. Again, the why is not important because resonance *is* and doesn't require a reason to be in existence other than the fact that it exists as an extension of Source.

You are your own sovereign and in unity with the Collective, the level of your frequency and respective light matters. *Self*-accountability comes into the dynamic between your sovereignty and your unification with the Collective because, "So, as the one (individual), as is the whole (Collective)." If you allow your vibration to be recurrently lowered by the static others create, you'll be in a constant state of non-resonance, which affects not only your frequency, but also that of the Collective.

If you are in a relationship that produces more non-resonance than it does resonance, you may be required to look inward and ensure you're accepting *what is*, which may be that the relationship, as a whole, is nonresonant. If the collection of your present moments in any given relationship is consistently requiring you to step out of the slipstream of joy, there may be a need for a greater assessment of *what is* within that relationship.

Part of grounding is re-rooting into new soil and retuning our frequency in the Natural is central to that process. Through this attunement, we will find that relationships either lift, shift, or drift. Meaning: your alignment awakens the ping of expression in another (lift); your retuned frequency allows the friendship to deepen while encouraging the other person to explore their authentic vibration (shift); or your elevated vibration will not find resonance due to the other person not being ready to awaken (drift).

If you have a relationship in the drift phase, stay in alignment with joy and send them an invitation for transformation from the heart. Many are in an unconscious state of suffering and if they drift away from you, it's not *because* of you. They are merely doing their best based on their current capacity to resonate—or not resonate—with Source and ultimately with that which they are born to express.

Just as a relationship is either resonant or nonresonant, situations or circumstances are either in or out of flow. As previously discussed, there is little value in attempting to understand why a relationship, situation, or circumstance is out of resonance or flow, seeing as those answers are immaterial to *what is*, which is the lack of resonance or flow. In navigating situations and relationships, the simplest principle by which to adhere is: frequency and Universal alignment have two states—resonance/flow or non-resonance/non-flow.

That is the guiding principle by which to keep static from interfering with the resonance of your vibration.

The alignment of earth and *going to ground* requires us to see *what is* in its entirety. We have been given an incredible opportunity for renewed vision and attunement, and it is here that we can come to realize that we don't have to suffer. We can live free in the slipstream of our expression if we'll only have the courage to go to ground and plant the first seed.

But before we plant, we must break ground—we must dig deep. Only then can the seed we have bravely planted be nourished by the water of our soul, cleansed by the air of our spirit, and warmed by the fire of our hearts.

HOW TO MOVE THE MOUNTAIN

Grid Focus: Self-assessment
Elemental Phase: I am but an earthbound seed.

- Again, step into the enchanted forest of your cognizance. Notice how lush and green the vegetation has become, as though being nourished by the essence of the earth.
- Listen to the forest's sounds and feel how deeply it longs to embrace you, grow around you—and *for* you.
- Carefully create the details of the circular path that leads you through the forest: What's on either side of the path? What kinds of flowers are growing there? What scents fill the air?
- As you walk, feel the soft earth beneath your bare feet. Know how deeply connected to the earth you are, and find gratitude for the grounding it affords.
- Let the refracted moonlight shining through the canopy of the trees bathe you in its magical[chemical] light.
- With each step, notice how much closer you feel to yourself. Immerse yourself within the sense of openness you exude—the sense of joy emanating from your cells.
- On your right, you see a magnificent oak tree and walk toward it.
- Take the time you need to really see its details: the

trunk, branches, leaves, and roots. Dive into your imagination and let the vision of the tree fill your mind's eye, along with your senses.

- Shift your focus to the tree's roots, some of which are python-sized and have broken through the forest floor. Notice how several of the roots come together, crisscrossing in a way that makes a perfect place for you sit and nestle into.

- After sitting, let your back rest against the trunk and feel the safety the tree offers; you haven't a care in the world. There is nothing but the forest, the oak, and you.

- Place your hands on the roots and feel the vibrant energy of the tree coursing through them; know that it is sentient and seeking communion with you.

- Now, reach down and take a bit of soil in each hand, letting its richness permeate your palms. Rub the soil in between your fingers and imagine all the forested treasures relying upon it for nourishment and growth.

- Take a deep breath and feel that this soil is nourishing you. At the base of the oak, nestled within its giant roots, consciously decide to go to ground. Allow your awakening to take hold and infiltrate your soul. Feel the seed of possibility manifest in your hand and stay with the sensation of cradling it in your palm as long as possible.

CHAPTER ELEVEN

Beauty in the Beast

PREVIOUSLY, WE TOUCHED UPON the importance of knowing all the matter that makes you, you. Meaning, a fundamental part of the grounding process—seeding your own earth—is understanding that your light is comprised of varying shades. Many of us spend our lives attempting to suppress the portions of ourselves we feel contain the darker shades. Yet shadow, or what we consider darkness, is nothing to be feared or vanquished.

There is a spectrum of matter in all things, seeing as without it, our existence would be one-dimensional, rather than omni-dimensional. The range of light inside our humanistic profile and vibrational frequency—our light spectrum—simply *is* because by its very nature, light is prismatic.

Illustratively, let's take our current walk through the forest: its beauty isn't in any way diminished by the fact that within our forest scene, it's night. If anything, the moonlight and the enchanted nature of its refracted light through the tree canopy only *add* to the forest's allure. The moon sending down its gentle glow and bathing the trees and forest floor in watery indigo light is a perfect parallel to understanding how the light spectrum exhibits within us.

Night brings forth an entirely different subset of creatures: nocturnal animals that need the darkness to preserve their preferred way of life. And just because these animals live by the light of the moon, they are no less valuable to the forest's ecosystem. In fact, the cycle of life would be severely impacted if the forest's nocturnal inhabitants were eliminated, as widespread imbalance would ensue.

The nocturnal aspect of the forest's ecosystem offsets the heat of the sun and provides a time of rest for the animals that are active during the day. This bionetwork is a streamlined symbiotic partnership that requires delicate balance to maintain its systemic integrity. Akin to the forest's dependence on both day and night, we require both light and dark to preserve our alchemical and ionic balance.

Seeing as darker light is widely misunderstood, we spend much of our lives pushing it down and in some cases, over-functioning in our brighter light spectrum to the point of damaging our connection to *Self*. Instances of this scenario can be seen in behaviors such as unremitting kindness, overt and regularly displayed humility, obsessive puritanical views, or unchecked generosity bordering on disingenuousness, to name a few.

What we often fail to realize is that through our connection to collective consciousness and unification with the Grid, we are communicating via our frequency at all times; we are constantly broadcasting a signal, and that vibrational wave carries information about our energy and intentions.

Consciously or unconsciously, others know when we're not truthful or authentic. They know if we like or dislike them and more importantly, they know if we're hiding a part of ourselves we don't want them to see. It's not uncommon to hear statements such as: "Something's off about him/her"; "I know he/she said they were fine, but my gut tells me otherwise"; "He/she is almost too nice"; "He/she makes me uncomfortable for some reason"; "There is something about him/her I just don't trust."

Our gut reads the darker aspects of light and lets us know when there's darkness in a frequency we're being sent. The gut doesn't alert us because there *is* darkness—it signals us because there is *covered* darkness attempting to masquerade as light. The engine of our intuition knows that covered darkness actively manipulated by a person sending us a signal is potentially unstable or *unequalized*.

Equalization is something that will naturally occur once elemental alignment is complete and in large part, it began after the activation of the violet flame. The process of equalizing sees us incorporating the entire spectrum of our light into our ionic structure and humanistic profile, meaning we're bringing darker light aspects into our resonant cognizance.

Prior to equalization, our tendency is to cover our darker light, which is behavior learned through either familial environments or socialization channels. We're taught and societally pressured to show only the sides of us that others deem acceptable and beautiful. As a result, we project a curated version of our light that fails to include our darkness—our depth.

In this, we displace a piece of ourselves and *Self*-shame until the darker light inside us is squelched to the point of becoming isolated. It is here that the darker matter in our spectrum is locked away like a prisoner for simply being what it *is*. Darker light doesn't know what color it is, nor does it care. Its only conscious impulse is to fulfill its place within the spectrum of our being: dark matter, in and of itself, is not negative or bad—it's simply light consisting of particles that reflect richer shades.

The result of *Self*-shaming and light curation causes our darker light to become entombed, which can manifest in the humanistic profile as displacement and urge fixation. Because the light has been isolated from the rest of the spectrum, it distorts and twists in on itself in an ultimate display of imbalance. Then, that distortion selects a fixed point of focus in which to forcefully disentomb itself.

In keeping with our earlier illustration, it would be akin to a forest experiencing only night, whereby the trees, plants, and flowers slowly wither and die while the nocturnal creatures begin taking over and altering the balance of the forest's ecosystem. Without a fulcrum of balance, the nocturnal animals overrun the barren forest until they eventually cannibalize one another. And here, we see a once-harmless animal transform into a ravenous beast.

In the Natural (physical plane), this *beast* will manifest in areas where light in our electromagnetic field has been displaced, or in areas where we originally *Self-*shamed. As an example, imagine a young man fascinated with antique dolls: they are to him what a Picasso may be to someone else; they are his version of high art.

At some point during his socialization, he recognizes that most other young men are not at all interested in dolls, antique or otherwise, and in so learning, he begins to *Self*-shame in order to foster acceptance with a broader group. During this process, he pushes down his fascination with his version of high art and the vibration of shame begins attaching to descriptors like *weird*, *gross*, or *abnormal*.

In some instances, others impose such descriptions upon us, but on many occasions, we taunt, label, and ostracize ourselves. Since shame attracts the darkest light in our spectrum, it will gather at a fixed point, often presenting as an idea, impulse, or set of thought patterns. Once that darker light attaches, it displaces the brighter light once present until the spectrum—as a whole—is imbalanced, and this is where innocent *potential* expression is contorted into a *beast*.

Whereas our young man may have become a world-renowned artisan doll maker, sought after by celebrities and collectors—an artistic pursuit that could well have been his true expression if explored—he now feels the need to cover or entomb what he considers a darker interest, or urge; this evidenced by shaming internal dialogue bordering on *Self*-abuse and predatory castings: "Only girls play with dolls"; "Something's wrong with me"; "I must be weird/abnormal/strange."

With darkness having gathered around an idea or thought pattern that he is abnormal or weird for having an interest in dolls, over time, he will have created a ravenous beast. Originally, his artistic impulse was light-filled and balanced on the spectrum. Now we see him overcompensating, while his masculinity falls prey to his beast until, in his bitterness, he succumbs to the impulse to bully, belittle, and dominate not only others but also himself.

Instead of accepting his interest in artisanship, which was most likely his true expression, he pushed down and entombed the darker light attached to the shame of his artistic curiosity being dolls. What we need to glean from this example is that dolls were never the actual expression; rather, it was *artistry* and the magical[chemical] fascination with creating that aligned him with joy and that which he was born to express. The dolls were the outlet—the artistry was the expression.

Potentiality was seeking him on the light spectrum and rather than accepting his attraction to artistry, he covered and pushed down what he assumed was a darker impulse associated with the dolls. Our young man, in his joy, wished to mold and create with the power of his hands: a magician with clay. Instead of trusting the truth of his expression and accepting the shades of the colors inside him, he covered and entombed a portion of his light, thereby creating his beast.

Yet our young man is not alone; we all have beasts. And no matter how ravenous our beasts, they're also our beauty, as they carry within them the truth of our expression and the depth of our colors. If we will but listen, our beasts will reveal the secrets of our light and the mysteries of our very selves.

CRY WOLF

Standing on a quiet path in the forest, you feel the colors of light in your spectrum awakening and attuning. The earth beneath your feet is becoming warmer, as though welcoming you into the splendor of the forested oasis supporting your cognizance and alignment.

In having gone through burn-off and the initiation of healing untended wounds, we're able to release the anger, rage, and encompassing fury we had previously suppressed. Merging our fire and fueling the violet flame has given us access to the grace and poise necessary to move deeper into the forest of ourselves, and thus, closer to that which we are born to express.

Similarly, aligning with the element of earth—or going to ground—requires tilling our earth and digging up the weeds and tangled roots that may eventually choke the seeds of our expression. But first, we need to understand that the richest soil is created by mixing aerated earth with what has expired or passed from one form to another.

Nature constantly utilizes the cycle of life as nourishment for its evolution; therefore, nothing really dies—it only changes form and purpose. Fallen leaves and fruit provide sustenance to the forest floor, while the passing of animals and insects fosters a nutrient-rich source to the progression of renewing life. Aligning with the element of earth sees us beginning to understand that life, like *Time*, is both circular and conscious.

As we grow in cognizance, we become aware that our life, the Force within us, has its own consciousness and is consistently attuning with the frequency of inspiration. Meaning, we are being guided and we are on the right path at all times, no matter how lost within the forest of ourselves we may seem. In this, know the Force within you is greater and more vigilant than any of the forces outside you; nothing can pull you from the path of your expression.

Distilled, this means that in coming into elemental alignment, we recognize that our cognizance draws toward us what we need. It understands that things must expire in order to make room for new growth, that we need to move through a sharp bed of rocks in order to shed skin, that we need to endure a hard rain to soak a parched spirit, and that we must climb the most unforgiving of mountains in order to gain a panoramic view.

In the spirit of exploration and engaging our imagination and magic—the ultimate fusion of the hemispheres in our brain and the duality in our physical and Universal journey—we are best served giving our beasts the freedom to roam the forest, uncaged. We can call them forth, giving them an imagined form with which to be disentombed from the catacombs we have built for them; we can unseal the tomb doors and let them walk out into the night.

So, let us call our beasts. Let us see them emerge from their tombs as we embrace the ravenousness of their spirits. We are powerful enough to listen to their voices, to tame them, and most importantly, to receive them. And as we open our hearts and send the signal of release, we hear the tomb doors unseal and watch in awe as they gather around us: they are our light, our dark, our poise, and our grace—they are our wolves.

They emerge from the shadows of the forest like an army representing our spectrum of light, some bearing fur of the brightest white and others of the blackest black; yet regardless of their color, they are ours. In giving them form and presence, we have set them free and allowed them the opportunity to see us, so as to receive the acceptance they have long been without.

Each of them wears an iron collar, a sign of us chaining them down by way of shaming ourselves into believing they deserved to live in darkness. In this moment, we kneel into the soft earth and with our heart, soul, and spirit cosmically charged and connecting to Source light, we receive them. One by one, we unchain them as they tell us and show us who they are, in turn we discover the beauty and nuances of their varying shades of light.

We find ourselves in admiration of their wisdom and ability to vibrate with Source frequency. And above all else, we feel the love emanating from them as they continue greeting us and sharing their stories. Our wolves are aspects of ourselves and we cannot experience wholeness until they are given the freedom they have earned; they are deserving of their place within the spectrum of light, and it's only by disentombing them that we will step into full and absolute equalization.

With our darker shades of light now released, we begin feeling our frequency growing increasingly resonant because in freeing our wolves—our beasts—we have unchained ourselves from the dungeon-like labyrinth of expectation. A partial impetus for creating our wolves was because, in one way or another, we felt out of sync with either what was expected of us from others or what we expected of ourselves.

Expectation lies at the root of the humanist profile, which has its own form of consciousness. Like our wolves, the humanistic profile is programmed to survive at all costs, yet the instinct that drives it isn't primal but liminal. The humanistic profile is consistently at the threshold of something greater than itself, which is Source light. But a connection to Source requires that the humanistic profile elevate to Source frequency, which can be likened to a software upgrade wherein the old data is written over with new code.

Our trinity knows this elevation is optimal and will ultimately bring us closer to that which we are born to express, but the humanistic profile is fiercely holding on to its older binary code. As a mode of circumvention, the humanistic profile uses expectation as a tool to make it *appear* we're elevating without actually accepting the overwrite.

The humanistic profile, in conjunction with us having created our wolves, attempts to push us into mainstream acceptance via expectation's bullying frequency: "You shouldn't have said that"; "You could have handled that better"; "You're not reaching your potential"; "You need to stop doing that." Yet, notice there isn't actually a directive here. There's only the *appearance* of awareness and the expectancy of acceptance and growth.

Therefore, the humanistic profile has made you think you are increasing your awareness and connection to Source by pointing out areas where you're falling below expectancy. However, know that the humanistic profile chooses its scale of expectancy based on what it experiences on the physical plane—meaning, until elevation, it's completely uninformed at a Source, Grid, and Collective level.

In going back to the example of our young man and his artisan dolls: he *Self*-shames his artistic impulse due in part to believing that his interests are falling below, or out of, expectation with what other young men—or society—find acceptable. Sample internal dialogue for this scenario may be: "You need to be more mature"; "You're not acting like other young men"; "You need to let go of this childishness"; and other such statements of expectation.

These declarations of expectation differ from the ego and will in that they are forming from the root of our humanistic profile. In keeping with our software metaphor, we can say that the humanistic profile *is* the operating software, whereas the will and ego are programs *within* the operational system that rely upon its broader code to run. And there is a thread of dependence between them, but it's a very minor line of code, seeing as the will and ego are programs that have their own self-invested and independent areas of purpose.

In having elevated all the prismatic aspects of your being, the humanistic profile will take care of its own upgrade in response to cognizance opening the door to (w)holistic elevation and alignment. At this point, the humanistic profile can no longer *appear* to be something it's not, and in releasing the wolves, the expectation partially responsible for entombing them has been revealed as falsified code.

Now, the humanistic profile must accept the reassembled spectrum of light and the pure and light-fueled Source code accompanying equalization and elemental alignment. With this unification, expectation is overwritten by elevation and reprogramed to resonate in the physical plane with that which you are born to express.

The disentombing of our wolves and resulting reintegration of the darker shades in our light spectrum have restored our *Self* into a state of Source origin. Understanding that the humanistic profile's use of expectation contributed to the entombment of our darker light, we bring our humanness into the slipstream of our cognizance, which fully aligns us with the Law of Amplitude.

With elevation in process, we recognize the merging of that which we are born to express cannot take place until we know our wolves—they are the keepers of our shadows and all that we are and will be. They accept us for who we are without judging our darker aspects and allow us a safe place to explore the deeper shades of our light. The knowledge our wolves carry is essential, for within it are the secrets we hide from ourselves. If, through the resonance of elemental alignment, we have the courage to ask them, our wolves will open the door to our expression.

Knowing we are at the precipice of elevation and amplitude, we look into the faces of our wolves and ask them what we need to know. We listen from soul to cells and let them teach us how to become one with the spectrum of light inside us. Then, in the forest of ourselves, we rise from our knees and continue our Walk with our wolves at our side, knowing that it is through our shadow that we will reclaim our light.

HOW TO MOVE THE MOUNTAIN

Grid Focus: Self-assessment
Elemental Phase: I am but an earthen path.

- In all the self-assessments thus far, this should be your most visceral. This is not only about the images in your mind's eye, but also about how you feel.
- Begin feeling the elements align and unify. Know you are elevating because you *feel* the vibration inside you.
- Take time to look out into the beautiful forest around you. See every moonlit tree, flower, and vine. Build the forest in your mind so thoroughly that you actually catch the scent of pine and blooming flowers in the air.
- Let the beat of your heart fall in time with each step until you can no longer distinguish between the sound of your footsteps and the beating of your heart.
- On either side of you are your wolves. Their ears are up and perked; they are there to guide and protect you.
- Gently, reach out and let your hand graze the fur of one of your wolves. Feel the softness of its fur and how it longs to stay connected with you. Notice the protectiveness you feel for its safety, its happiness, and its life.
- Then let yourself connect to all of them, deeply and truthfully. This is your pack created by you to cover

all the darker light you thought needed concealing. And understand now that you want nothing more than for your wolves to run free, to live in the varying shades of light they represent.

- On your right, one of the wolves has slowly wandered off the path and has begun to dig. Eventually, all the wolves scatter throughout the forest and follow suit. You notice they are calm yet determined as they uproot old weeds and patches of deadened vegetation.

- Innately, you recognize that they are tilling soil and preparing your spectrum of light to unify, while fostering the planting of new seeds.

- Breathing steadily, you become aware of the wholeness you feel; as though all of you are ready to stand in the light.

- Finding yourself on a patch of hardened ground, you join them and begin to dig, tilling the soil until it transforms into soft earth. The sacredness you feel as you realize you have the power to make barren soil seed-ready resonates into your soul like water to parched earth.

CHAPTER TWELVE

Half Light

THE ESSENCE OF FIRST LIGHT falls on the forest while you survey the newly tilled soil of the forest floor. The scent of fresh earth permeates the air as you notice the surrounding trees beginning to release cottony seeds that rain down like winter snow.

Although the air is laced with night's chill, you can feel the coming dawn and the warmth it brings. The wolves have fanned out into the forest in an effort to continue tilling soil, leaving you alone to enjoy the peace of having reintegrated the spectrum of your light into your Source-filled being.

The Collective calls to you and welcomes your elevated frequency, and as you receive the resonant vibration, you understand how profound the sense of

Oneness feels. It's all-encompassing, like a great net of protection and guidance that infiltrates every cell and tonal thread in your frequency. This is belonging personified, and it is here that you truly comprehend the *you-nity* in Oneness.

In reintegrating the spectrum of your light, you have begun accepting all the different shades of who you are and what you will become; you understand that your light is not without its indigos and darker colors. Yet in seeing the spectrum through the eyes of your omni-dimensional spirit, you've embraced the oceanic hues that make you who you are.

Untended wounds are healing and being cauterized by the violet flame of your heart, while the pull of your will, ego, and mind fades into the background like watercolor scenery. At the forefront of your soul is the base element of grace, which calls upon you to anchor the Source fuel of your soul into the humanistic profile. This process is rooting you into your newly aligned state and preparing you to receive that which you are born to express.

The soul carries within it the encoded light of Source and Grid and for those of us remaining unawakened, the fullness of the soul's capacity would overpower the density of our humanistic profile. Once burn-off, spectrum integration, and elemental alignment are underway, the process of elevation raises the vibration of the humanistic profile to the point that it can accept a greater level of the soul's Source-fueled light.

Rooting the soul deeper into the humanistic profile takes you from the core functionality of a one-dimensional structure into the optimized experience of omni-dimensional carbon-encased light. In the former, you are bound to primal and sub-primal impulses, whereas in the latter, you are freed by the prismatic and electro-ionic beams of light that radiate photonic waves capable of altering the fabric of spatial formation.

The aligning elements in conjunction with the infusion of spectrum light will open a channel to receive the full Source-fueled frequency of the soul, which will result in a humanistic profile comprised of phyto-cellular versus bio-cellular material. This is why the element of earth is crucial for rooting the soul into the humanistic profile, because at a cellular level, you are becoming light-activated. As with the photosynthesis in plants, you too—as the root of the word indicates—will *synthesize light*.

This shift from bio-organic to photo-organic means that you are stepping into the fullness of *light experiencing being human*. You are not losing any of your humanness; rather, you are shedding the denser aspects of the humanistic profile that interfere with the frequency of joy.

Your soul harnesses atomic-level combustion potential, but because it's Source-fueled and contains a nucleus of the base element grace, there is zero volatility. Instead, the atomic combustion of the soul can be used to alchemically alter the vapor-like strands of spatial formation and your physical environment.

In rooting the soul into the humanistic profile and allowing the entire light-bearing weight of the soul in, we are altering the way in which we will interact with, and manifest, reality. We will no longer be in a reactive relationship with our reality—we will be in an interactive partnership with our alchemy. Our atomic combustion will combine with our elevated frequency until we can mold spatial formation and its environmental counterparts into manifested form; quite literally, we become artists forming the clay of our lives.

Rooting provides the launch pad for that which we are born to express, by giving it the atomic power to manifest in an elementally aligned environment. The cottony white seeds falling to the ground around you are pieces of your soul that will take root in the tilled earth, then spread outward in a network supporting the forest of you.

These networked light- and soul-infused roots pulse with atomic light that ionically charge the base of our consciousness while raising our frequency of awareness. Once the rooting is complete, we will experience and see circumstances differently due to the alteration of our cellular structure; a bio-cellular makeup only permits us to see at a bio-molecular level, but a phyto- and photo-molecular makeup gives us a form of Xray vision into our environment.

Seeing and experiencing the world around us through a light frequency while rooting deeper into our soul activates compassion for not only ourselves but others. Once experiencing our environments from a light frequency of resonant joy, we will understand the pain others experience when bound by the density of the humanistic profile. And for them, we will resound with compassion and recognize the suffering and soul debris keeping them from resonating at the level of their expression.

Here we meet them and share enough light to awaken within them the spark of curiosity and the ignition of remembrance. Then, by merely coming into contact with an awakened and rooted soul, their spirit sends the ping of Source light to their heart, until their elemental alignment begins.

The Law of the Collective states: "The light of one is the light in all. Nothing is separate nor undeserving of alignment. All souls, for the sole Oneness. It is and shall remain." During the process of rooting, we gain access to the pooled resources of the Collective—meaning, we share atomic force and the ability to alter spatial orientation.

Therefore, when enough of us awaken, we'll be able to alter the course of humanity, if we so choose. This is not science fiction, nor is it societally driven pseudo-religion; it is Source truth. For why would the Source of all light force us to live in the shadows of darkness without empowering us to free our souls, ourselves? Source wouldn't and hasn't.

In many ways, we have always had the *key to the kingdom*, but in the case of humanity, each individual carries a piece of the key and must align with the greater whole in order for the key to be assembled and put to use. This is the function of the Collective: "All for one, in harmony with unity and collectively purposed to express—there is only this, and it is unchanging."

Claiming the piece of our key in order to serve the greater whole requires us to come into alignment with that which we are born to express. This is where we elevate the humanistic profile to the threshold of *becoming* light: it is where flesh leaves the density of its organic compounds and inhabits the frequency of its compounded light.

When fully rooted, you will be able to alter the fundamental aspects of your environment, which calls for radical *Self*-accountability. In wielding that kind of power, you have a responsibly to your fellow souls, both awakened or unawakened. You cannot, in any way, abuse this atomic light, or like sun to mirror, you will inflict harm upon yourself. Such an occurrence is not to be confused with what some misperceive as the law of karma; rather, what we're addressing is the reflective capacity of the fabric of spatial formation.

The Universe and its respective surroundings are comprised of the matter making up all that is, or the fabric of spatial formation and capacity, which is comprised of interwoven light. If we could see this fabric in its true state, we wouldn't see empty blackness; instead, we'd see an infinite web of light. Elemental alignment and the rooting of the soul give us access to light perception that laid dormant in the unrooted humanistic profile. But in having integrated our spectrum of light and opened the channel to our Source-fueled souls, we are integrally bound by the reflective capabilities of the Universe's spatial fabric.

Our light makes contact with the fabric and returns to us within the same frequency it was sent. So, whereas karma centers on a corrective process by which others inflict our supposed karmic debts (which don't actually exist), the reflective nature of spatial fabric and formation simply reflects the light we're emitting. Thereby, keeping accountability where it belongs, which is with *Self*, seeing as it is never about another person: we are solely responsible and in relationship with our *Self*.

Within this infinite web of light lies the magical clay awaiting the Source-powered agility of your soul-filled hands. Once the process of rooting is complete, you will be ready to fully receive that which you are born to express. Until then, while awaiting the network of your forest to root and grow, you reunite with your earthen path as you watch the approaching violet dawn.

Bathed in the half light of night and day, you feel the earth moving beneath your feet as the roots below ground tunnel and connect you to your soul. Having seeded your earth with the breath of creation, you can begin to feel the flicker of Source spark warming the air around you as you await the truth and lightness of your expression.

THE WILD ROSE

While dawn continues illuminating the forest in violet light, you find that your path leads to a perfectly circular meadow. Flower-covered and magical in its detail, you walk into the meadow feeling as though you're home. The trees surrounding the meadow are majestic in both stature and presence, and were you to close your eyes, you'd swear you were encircled by the essence of Source itself.

In this enchanted place and rooted in your soul, you wield the atomic power of light at your fingertips. Every part of your body is charged with photonic pulses that infiltrate your blood, stoking the violet flame of your heart while stirring your oceanic depths and windswept lightness into one streaming and cohesive current.

You are light embodied, and the frequency of the Collective rings so clearly in your spirit that you can feel its resonance penetrating your cells. The elements within you fuse into a single unified circle, with each element inhabiting a quadrant: four pieces become one, just as you unify with the Collective, the whole. And in both element and humanness, you fully align with Oneness.

The Law of Amplitude attunes to the frequency of joy and transforms the woven fabric of spatial formation into a reflection of all that you are. There is nothing between you and your expression now; fusion is imminent, just as your alchemical transfiguration is permanent.

Your courage has seen you deep-dive into the ocean of your soul, reach the gusty mountain peak of your spirit, merge the fires of your heart, then seed and root the earth of your cognizance. In equalizing and integrating the light of your spectrum, you have purified the connection to Source and the Grid, in turn unifying with the vibration of the Collective.

In aligning the elements, you're resonating at the highest frequency possible while attuning to that which you are born to express. This meadow is a place for you to hone and practice your magicianship, as you continue to attune to your expression; it will teach you the pure principles of harmonic and symbiotic resonance.

The meadow is made up of living things integrating and becoming one, whereby everything must align to a frequency honoring the greater whole, so as to foster grace and poise. While breathing in the meadow's floral scent, you notice a vibrantly red—and undoubtedly wild—rose in the center of the meadow.

As though compelled by something outside yourself, you walk toward it. With a thick stem and razor-sharp thorns, the rose appears formidable but as you grow closer, you feel it wants you near—it needs you near.

Now standing in front of the rose, you kneel and examine its silky crimson petals, which are open and emitting an intoxicating scent. It seems the rose's tiny veins are electrically charged, seeing as every few seconds, you notice a surge of white light running through its petals.

You feel the rose is alive and conscious and if you listen closely enough, you can almost hear it speak. In a voice of resonant harmony, you understand that the rose is your expression: wild, free, and deeply rooted. You are here to cultivate the rose of your expression until such time as you may yield the attunement it brings.

First, the rose needs the elements aligned: water for thirst, earth for nourishment, air to breathe, and the violet light of your forest's sun to grow. Any one element overtaking another chokes the rose's growth; but in balance, the elements will cradle the wildness of the rose's beauty and coax it into bloom.

Within the metaphor of the rose, we see the delicate aspects of its petals and the fierceness of its thorns, in that it has learned to adapt to the tumultuous environments it's endured to be near you. Yet the rose is far from fragile and if tended and attuned, it will give its lifeblood to fuse with its gardener: you.

This is the seed of your expression and having grown, it now reaches toward the light. Here, in the magic of the meadow, you are safe to cultivate and bloom that which you are born to express. By the sight of the rose, you will know both the state of your connection to Source and the resonance of your elemental alignment, as all will be revealed by the fullness of the rose's bloom.

This wild rose is not of you—it *is* you, because you

are your expression. In tending to its bloom, you will elevate your resonance with *Self* and understand the importance of attuning to its frequency. You are your own gardener, and it is at your hand that your rose will either wither or bloom.

The bravery you have shown in coming this far has taken the rose from once-barren land and replanted it in the majestic meadow of your grace-filled frequency. You must spend time reacquainting with the wildness of your spirit while attuning to the melodic vibration of Source.

Let your untended wounds complete the last stages of healing as the final pieces of your soul take root. Past stories of pain have no power over you now, nor will they ever again be able to access the inner chambers of your violet-flamed heart. Your sovereignty over *you* reigns supreme and resonates within the choral harmony of the Universe.

Knowledge, as with air, is breathed in as you access the wisdom of the Collective and call upon the support of Oneness. The Grid resonates with the consciousness of your expression and funnels that current into the rose. And while you lay in the meadow and let the beauty inside you radiate like the sun, you feel the light-bearing signal of Source coursing through your veins. So it is and so it shall always be: you, in the joy of your expression. You are the light of the world, the still in the night, and the bloom of the wild rose.

HOW TO MOVE THE MOUNTAIN

Grid Focus: Self-assessment
Elemental Phase: I am but a wild rose.

- This assessment will be self-led, as it's important you go deep within your *Self*, by yourself.
- As a place to begin: stay in the meadow and let your imagination run wild. Give yourself time to play and hone your magicianship without boundaries or judgment.
- Feel the current of your expression coursing through you as you come into bloom and know that fusion with your expression is imminent.

The Elemental

"There is no logical way to the discovery of these elemental laws. There is only the way of intuition, which is helped by a feeling for the order lying behind the appearance."
—ALBERT EINSTEIN

CHAPTER THIRTEEN

Sand to Stardust

THE JOURNEY OF THE GRID WORK has opened the channel to our expression. We are steeped in light and our humanistic profile has been elevated and rooted by our soul. There has been an alchemical change in our cellular and ionic structure that will continue to refine as we move toward fusing with our expression.

Once the soul, heart, and spirit are fully aligned, they will work to refine and attune with Source frequency. The humanistic profile will elevate into the vibration of the Collective as our mind accesses a deeper sense of understanding who we are at a cosmic level. Core wounds lose their hold on our humanness while the violet flame in our heart burns cleaner and stronger.

In having reintegrated the spectrum of our light, the prismatic aspects of our trinity will bring the quadrants of our elements into wholeness and balance. This unification will activate the inter-elemental relationships within our humanistic profile, which can then offer an equalized platform for that which we are born to express.

The attunement journey and subsequent elevation of our humanistic profile can provide rapid succession toward our expression, yet that is the exception rather than the rule. Oftentimes, what first transpires is the shedding of soul-deadening debris along with the quieting of the noise generated by the mind. Once our unique frequency receives an open channel in which to resonate, it will connect to Source vibration and commence unification with that which we are born to express.

There is an attraction principle to consider, in that the signal of our expression will magnetically align with amplification, which is now active in both our cosmic and auric fields; in essence, our energy can be likened to a colossal satellite dish sending and receiving Source frequency through a focused point of atomic-powered light.

Although our frequency and relationship with the Law of Amplitude have entered into our consciousness, there is a soul component to attunement that works within the unconscious. Meaning, in accepting the unification of the elements within us, we have given our spirit license to work independently of the humanistic profile for the sole purpose of continually elevating our frequency.

Self-accountability will be crucial in the attunement and amplification phases, seeing as our frequencies will no longer be capable of resonating at lower levels. Situations, relationships, and scenarios that were once attuned may no longer be in resonant space, which is a byproduct of alignment and not one to be judged or assessed from the recesses of primal emotions.

This doesn't require us to lock out how we feel about the shifts in our natural lives, but it does encourage us to engage with the alterations of our vibrations in an aligned manner. Changes in the profiles of our relationships are to be expected and should stay in the experiential plane of the heart.

For example, if you were walking down a glorious path with a trusted friend and you came to a fork in the road, there is a choice: travel together in both spirit and body, or honor a physical departure that keeps the spirits aligned. Imagine your companion states that they would like to explore the right side of the path and the tall trees that reside there, whereas you would rather walk the left path with its surrounding botanical gardens.

The friend's desire to spend time amongst the trees is not personal, nor does it indicate how they feel about you—it's simply where they are resonating at that *Time*. In your respective spirits, you can stay in unity while understanding that separating physically is necessary in order to honor each other's needs. Therefore, with your vibrational frequency attuning to Source, you may find yourself traveling without them; but this doesn't mean they are lesser than or deserving of judgment in any way. It simply indicates that they have chosen a different fork in the road. Yet, know that the elevation of your frequency will have profoundly affected them and perhaps even ignited the alignment with that which they are born to express.

Energy is fluid by Universal law and with this as truth, what the humanistic profile views as change is a fundamental given. Universal fluidity is constant and prismatic in its current, and its resulting ebb and flow is one of the most exquisite aspects of its function. Ever in motion, Universal current keeps regeneration, purity, and flow available to us at all times; without it, we would lose our connection to the Source spark of creation.

While aligning and attuning to that which we are born to express, we fluctuate in resonance: relationships and situations once in resonance may now be in non-resonance, whereas relationships and situations once in non-resonance may enter into a period of resonance. The balance point is in the elements within us; they are the key to balancing and elevating the humanistic profile while attuning to Source frequency. Our elements form our inner Force, which is the strike point of light inside us that activates our magicianship and alchemical abilities.

Heightened emotions trap the current within our humanistic profile, which requires us to be diligent while in the adjustment cycle of our natural lives. This doesn't mean you don't *feel* the shifts in resonance within relationships and circumstances—it simply means you don't place judgments upon what you're feeling or allow it to inform action in the Natural.

In practice, if in non-resonance with a relationship, allow the feelings to arise but don't block their ability to flow and inform alignment. Even non-resonance has its own manner of flow, as it's still an energetic current; the only difference between resonance and non-resonance is in the information they carry. Therefore, it's the information with which you stay in alignment, rather than the emotion or judgment specific to the circumstance.

In picking up with our earlier illustration regarding two travelers taking different forks in a path, we understand that the other person wanting to explore the trees rather than the flowers doesn't make them bad. The *information* carried in this circumstance is that we are not in directional resonance with that spirit at this time. Although we may have feelings about their departure, we accept that they are attuning to that which they are born to express, and that resulting sojourn may not include us—at least, not at this time.

Being elemental means that when the fire of the heart ignites due to someone going in a different direction, we temper that fire with earth and send attunement flow and support to them as they seek to seed their own expression. Similarly, when the water of emotion rushes toward us and tears through our humanistic profile

THE ELEMENTAL

when we experience a relationship shift, we call in the wisdom of the wind to calm our stormy sea and bring us back to the base of our mountain.

The elements within us are tools for mastering the Universal alchemy of our cosmic field. We can liken the relationship to a remote-control device informing the movements of a larger object: our elemental abilities are directly connected to the cosmic aspects of our alchemy and magicianship. Meaning, if we are elementally misaligned, we cannot inform the movement and flow of our magic and Source-powered alchemy. This is why the rooting of the soul into the humanistic profile is vital, because it is here that we anchor the light into the profile and ensure consistent elevation, in turn elemental alignment and the ability to utilize our magicianship and alchemical abilities.

Each of the elements within us has anchor points and archer points—an element can work for or against our greater alignment. As an illustration, we see how fire creates vivification in its ability to ignite, yet volatility in its ability to burn unchecked; how air is vital in its life-giving properties, yet volatile in its ability to level what's in its path; how earth is essential in its nourishment and grounding abilities, yet capable of burying and entombing; how water flows and fosters purity, yet can drown or stagnate.

The duality of our elements echoes the spectrum of our light—in all things, there are both light and

196

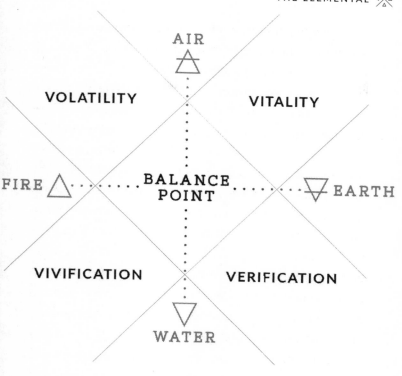

shadow. As a point of focus, we want to incorporate our acceptance of all that is for the purpose of all that can be, which means: we cannot resist even one aspect of our *Self* or our experience, or we resist *what is*. Using the elements as our balance point allows us to utilize the power of the quadrant filtration capabilities they possess, whereby everything we experience travels through a purification mechanism prior to our engagement with, or in, any given relationship, circumstance, or scenario.

The filter consists of the four elements surrounding the base element of grace, which is the portal to Source vibration and the intake point of everything we experience. In making this elemental filtration our primary point of contact with the Natural, we can attune all incoming frequencies prior to their integration into the deeper levels of our heart, soul, and spirit. Here, we find a platform of balance that keeps our humanistic profile in a state of alignment and resonant vibration because we have exchanged its primitive filter of mind, ego, and will with an alchemical filter—or portal—of the elements.

In any given circumstance, you can use the elemental portal to stay in flow and filter incoming frequencies so as to foster continued elevation in the humanistic profile. When you are met with incoming fire, it can be tempered with earth, and when you are met with a barrage of water, it can be countered with air, and so on. You can now use Source connection to harness magicianship and practice your alchemy and ability to manifest in the Natural.

Within the Natural and mental planes, your new balance point will consist of wonderment. Rather than forcing concepts upon your consciousness, such as happiness, fulfillment, or gratitude, you will simply resonate with the innate knowing that you are of Source.

Many exert a great deal of energy toward the concept of gratitude, which can bring certain aspects of

PRE-ELEVATION

NATURAL PLANE

POST-ELEVATION

NATURAL PLANE

MIND

HUMANISTIC
PROFILE

EGO   WILL

AIR

FIRE····▸GRACE◂··EARTH

WATER

FRENETIC FREQUENCY

BALANCED FREQUENCY

amplitude into their cosmic field. But what gratitude assumes is that you are a recipient; you are an individual to whom something is given. This implies that there is an external giver, or an energy to which you are beholden or reliant upon. From a frequency perspective, this is a lower vibration than Source light and fails to take into account the circular nature of Universal spatial formation.

Wonderment is the Source-level vibrational form of gratitude, in that wonderment encompasses circularity and the alchemical magicianship that is connately part of your cosmic, atomic, and ionic structure. There is no *given* or *giver*—there is only the light from which we are made, which consists of all that is. When in wonderment, we are aligned with Source and charging the flow of the light-infused magic already present in our structure: we are in awe of the alchemy we possess and in unity with alchemical Force. This is, and will always be, the Source of our expression and aptness of living.

Source seeks alignment and connection with pieces of itself, and it is here that we will always find a *home*. We are Source light created from the highest frequency in the Universe and in that, we can flow in wonderment; we can resonate in the magical spark of our existence. This state of being is far beyond gratitude, as it takes our awareness and kinship to a Universal alchemical level. From this viewpoint, we understand and begin to appreciate the trueness of our majesty, and this is where our expression can flow.

When aligned with our expression, we activate the light in others and give them the seed of wonderment to plant within their own respective forest. They sense our frequency and remember the light from which they are made; they come to realize they don't have to suffer and can transform sand to stardust. In unleashing our expression, regardless of how long it takes for us to do so, we are releasing the power of unity and lending an energetic hand to our brethren. This is the flow of the Collective and the coalition of light, and as a result, fusion with our expression is imminent.

Now, you can follow your path out of the forest where you went to ground, tilled your soil, rooted your soul, integrated your spectrum of light, met your wolves, and then met yourself. Violet dawn has turned into glorious light and as you leave the forest behind, you find yourself at the base of the mountain you recently climbed. Sending your gaze upward, you are in wonderment at the exquisiteness of the mountain: its earthen base, misted path, snowy peak, and fiery core, all comingling to form a perfectly balanced manifestation of elements.

In this moment, you realize that what the mountains know is *you*. You are their creator and their master. They are there *for* you, because *of* you. And had you not had the courage to climb this mountain's steep and mist-filled path and descend into its fiery core, you'd never have experienced the bravery of your spirit. Your mountains know—and will always seek to show you—how magical you really are.

LETTER FROM THE AUTHOR

This book came through me at a time of great personal suffering and uncertainty. There were times I didn't think I could take one more step or go one more day. In the valley of my shadows, as a person, I had never felt more misunderstood or unsupported. Struggling to find balance and centering within myself, I poured the wisdom of the writing into my own life.

I personally walked this path while slowly aligning with my true expression. The words in this book, in many ways, are inked in the blood I had to wade through to write them. But as I wrote, I listened to what was coming through and in opening that channel, I slowly began to heal.

For me, it's an honor to walk with you, and I stand in awe of your courage and bravery. This journey is powerful and profound, but I feel compelled to reach out to those of you who have experienced any kind of abuse or trauma, so as to offer support. If you are living with the effects of having survived abuse or trauma, to any degree or in any form, I encourage you to combine the Grid Work with psychotherapeutic care.

The Grid Work aligns *Self* and attunes you with Source frequency, but if you're carrying trauma in your physical body and mind, professional care can provide a level of support that allows the psyche to further unbind you from the story of your pain.

Unfortunately, society has attached a stigma of shame on psychotherapeutic care, but I feel it deserves addressing that you should give yourself what you need to be free. If you are a survivor, know that you are and will always be *light*. No one can take that from you, nor can they dim the magnificence within you.

You were not born to suffer, and you are not your story of pain. We are all in this together and it's vital you understand that within the light, you are loved, you are seen, and you are safe.

In Wonderment,
Shannon

ABOUT THE AUTHOR

SHANNON DENISE EVANS is a multidisciplinary artist, novelist, and life coach based in NYC. Between coaching others and her own personal experience, she believes we each possess a unique expression, one that is alchemically charged and designed to resonate within its own vibrational frequency. Her teachings center on the fact that we are not meant to suffer, rather we are designed to command the elements within us—we are born to be elemental, alchemical and to harness the magic of our expression.

· · · · · · · · · ·

CONNECT WITH THE AUTHOR
Facebook: @KnowURmountains
Twitter: @KnowURmountains
Instagram: @KnowURmountains
Email: *move@WhatTheMountainsKnow.com*
Web: *www.WhatTheMountainsKnow.com*

DESIGNER'S NOTE

This book is set in Palatino, designed by Hermann Zapf. Headlines are in Lato, by Łukasz Dziedzic. All photography in this book was sourced from Unsplash, an online library of professional photography available for free.

Made in the USA
Monee, IL
16 March 2020